Fundamentals of Offshore Banking

How To Open Accounts Almost Anywhere

by

Walter Tyndale

Pratzen Publishing

> ## "When goods cannot cross borders, armies will."
>
> -Frédéric Bastiat (1801-1850)

Legal Disclaimer

This publication provides information about international banking and includes references to certain legal and financial principles. Although the author and the publisher believe that the included information is accurate and useful, nothing contained in this publication can be considered professional advice on any legal or financial matter. You must consult a licensed attorney if you want professional advice that is appropriate to your particular situation. Where the information is to be relied upon by the user, the information should be independently verified.

Table of Contents

Why Offshore Banking?

Everyone is familiar with the "Offshore Bank Account". This term possesses a romantic mystique that is very appealing to many people. The term conjures up images of spies and international business moguls secretly hiding their wealth from the world.

However, the truth is that there are many legitimate and useful purposes to moving your money abroad. Many Europeans vacation in foreign countries and have banking relationships in those countries as well as in their home country. Money is the one truly portable asset in the world. Real estate, gold or cars cannot be moved without cost and effort. However, thanks to the advent of computer technology and electronic banking, you can move money around the world 24 hours a day with the click of a button. This allows you to take advantage of business opportunities, currency diversification, higher interest rates, favorable banking practices and the convenience of access to your money anywhere in the world.

Globalism is here to stay and as time passes, the world grows smaller. Businesses continue to expand onto the international level. There is a good chance that you may want to move your money abroad one day. Your business may involve you in travel overseas; you may retire abroad, or wish to diversify the currency of your savings. This book seeks to reveal the basic information that you will need to accomplish these goals.

Before we get started, I would like to state that I am not an expert on financial matters. It is true that you cannot make wise choices without knowing all of your options. This is the purpose of this work, to provide you, the reader, with a broad overview of the options available to you in the international banking community. With this information in hand, you can do further research specifically tailored to your personal situation in order to make proper, relevant and informed decisions.

When considering the movement of capital across international lines, there are many laws that you must abide by. You must always comply with all applicable laws, including the tax laws of your home country and the country you will be banking in. International banking should never be used to avoid taxes or hide money. Failure to comply with any laws of your country can result in the forfeiture of money, large fines and severe criminal penalties.

Each and every person is different and each person's situation is unique. For the most current and accurate information to your personal situation, always consult with a qualified, licensed attorney. No part of this work should be considered legal or financial advice. This work is provided for informational purposes only._

Traveling Abroad

Traveling abroad can be a truly rewarding, once in a lifetime experience. Mark Twain once wrote that "Travel is fatal to prejudice, bigotry and narrow-mindedness." However, for international travel to be truly enjoyable, you need to make sure that you have planned properly and are ready to go. One of the first steps in doing this is to ensure access to the financial resources that international travel can demand. Opportunities that demand more money than you had planned on can occur without warning. Even more alarming, disasters such as lost wallets, erased credit card magnetic strips and bank holds can appear suddenly. Sometimes, for no explainable reason whatsoever, foreign banks will not accept your ATM card or PIN code. This can leave you high and dry and force you to make embarrassing emergency calls to friends and relatives to have funds wired to you.

All of these headaches can be avoided by establishing a relationship with a local bank in the country or countries that you plan to visit. In the event of a problem occurring, nothing can be simpler or more reassuring than walking into a local branch in a foreign country and receiving personalized service as an established customer of record. Ask anyone who has ever changed their PIN code in a foreign country or walked into a bank and made a face to face withdrawal in the currency of their choosing and they will tell you the same.

For this reason, international banking is a subject with which you should be familiar. Additionally, due to their popularity as tourist destinations, many countries that are not considered "traditional offshore jurisdictions" are included in Chapter 5. These countries will permit their banks to open accounts for non-resident foreigners. However, you will have to find a bank whose internal policies will permit this.

Higher Interest Rates

Many foreign banks in developing nations are seeking capital to grow into larger banks and for local development resources. Banks in developing nations cannot make loans for construction projects that create jobs and strong economies if they do not have the money in their coffers to begin with.

To encourage foreign investment, the banks themselves will often offer higher interest rates than can be found in the developed world. Most often, these rates present themselves in the form of interest rates on certificates of deposit. This account forms will be discussed in Chapter 3 in detail. Sometimes, these rates can be quite high and may be worth the added risk to your deposit given your personal financial situation.

With all foreign banking deposits, it is important to remember that that the protections offered by the FDIC, or your home country's deposit insurance plan do not apply. Many of the developing countries that offer higher interest rates do not have deposit compensation plans, although some do. Always remember, that the higher the offered interest, the higher the implied risk to your deposit.

Added Privacy

Something that you will quickly learn in any exploration of the subject of offshore banking is that many foreign banks know how to be discreet. Banks in countries with developed offshore banking industries will not be constantly mailing you credit card applications or selling your information to others.

The Swiss banking system is the best known example of this discretion. In Switzerland, for example, there are strict bank secrecy laws in place to prevent the release of any customer's information. Swiss law does permit the release of information in compliance with a criminal investigation. This type of law is common in countries that actively seek offshore capital investments.

This discretion and dedication to the privacy of a bank's customers extends well beyond Switzerland. You can find similar systems in place all over the Caribbean, Europe and East Asia.

Bank privacy can be a wonderful thing. Many people prefer to keep matters concerning their wealth private and secret. However, there are limits to bank privacy that anyone considering offshore banking should be aware of.

Many foreign banks will rigorously defend you privacy and not release information, until they are requested to do so in relation to a criminal investigation. This includes tax evasion. Foreign banks have a vested interest in assuring that the transactions that they carry out are legitimate. Money laundering and other transactions relating to criminal activity put the whole concept of bank privacy in danger. As such, when asked to release information by a law enforcement agency, supported by proper legal documentation, international banks will comply.

You can also not use bank secrecy laws to hide money from the government to avoid paying taxes. <u>Don't even think about it</u>. Government agencies that are responsible for collecting taxes, such as the Internal Revenue Service, have long arms and good memories. In recent years, many government agencies have gone to great efforts to discover what is concealed in accounts around the world. In the United States, for example, owners of foreign bank accounts are required to notify the IRS of these accounts. (This will be discussed further in Chapter 2.) Hiding money in these accounts to avoid taxes is illegal and can land you in a great deal of trouble. Many countries around the world have been signing mutual tax information sharing treaties as well. This means that tax information is automatically available between countries. This is simply further incentive to make sure all of your international banking relationships are legitimate and in compliance with the law. Attorneys can help with this a great deal.

Lower Tax Zones

Many developing nations lack the capital necessary to form truly developed diversified economies, create jobs and improve the lives of their citizens. In order to do this, these countries need to attract large amounts of foreign investment.

It has already been discussed how governments and banks in these countries can help to encourage foreign investment by offering high rates of interest. These returns help to persuade investors that these riskier investments can be well worth the risk. However, there is another option open to governments alone that can greatly increase foreign investment as well as create jobs. This is tax policy management.

Many countries in the Caribbean have no personal, income, inheritance, sales, value added, capital gains or other taxes. They are not used by the government to support development or pay for day to day administration. Instead, these governments rely on tourist landing fees (cruise ships pay a fee for every passenger in every port they call in) or other revenue from the tourism industry to pay the bills.

Along with tourism, offshore finance provides another stream of revenue to the government in the form of corporate registration fees from banks and corporations established on the islands. The banks are drawn to the island by the low or no taxes that they know will encourage investors and other clients from around the world hoping to ease their tax burden. Corporations are also drawn to the islands by the hopes of adding to their bottom lines. Along with customers of the banks and corporations, wealthy retirees from abroad can also be encouraged to relocate to the islands by tax policies of this kind. Many of these people will have government or corporate backed pensions that can be spent locally and help to strengthen the economy as well.

This is the reason that many traditional offshore jurisdictions have a very high per capita amounts of registered corporations when compared with their citizenry. Additionally, many of the highest concentrations of wealth in the world are in very small countries with almost no taxation.

No matter what the tax policy of the countries in which you bank are, you must always comply with the tax policies of your home country. Offshore banking should never be used to avoid taxes. This is a crime. For the most competent advice and current information, consult a licensed attorney.

International Business Dealings

In the last few decades since the formation of the World Trade Organization (WTO) and the passage of North American Free Trade Agreement (NAFTA) and other trade agreements, there has been an explosion of world trade. Adding to this boom has been the economic development of emerging markets such as India and China.

Every day, billions of dollars in goods and services travel across international boundaries. New products are exported and imported and new technologies are developed.

In order to carry out international business, companies will often use letters of credit or credit accounts. However, there are potential advantages to having an existing relationship with a bank in the country where business will be transacted. You can carry out immediate transfers and establish lines of credit to help manage cash flow and ensure the uninterrupted flow of goods.

Additionally, if you have any need of escrow services, banks in the manufacturer's home country can be very convenient.

International Business Companies

Many businesses will have banking relationships with local banks in the foreign countries where they conduct business. Many individuals and companies choose to go one step further and incorporate in foreign countries. These offshore corporations are frequently referred to as "international business companies" or more simply, "IBCs".

The subject of incorporation is an amazingly complicated one. When you add the twist of incorporating in a foreign country, the subject becomes so intricate that only attorneys should attempt to explain it and are equipped to carry out an overseas incorporation. The offshore jurisdictions that specialize in the establishment of IBCs will be well stocked with qualified attorneys capable of helping clients through the process.

Forming a corporation in a foreign country offers many advantages. Firstly, many of the countries that have international banking centers that specialize in IBCs, have very low, if any taxes. This means that you may be able to lower the taxes from business profits by forming a corporation overseas. This is another reason that these areas are often called tax havens. Again, before funneling any money overseas and establishing a foreign corporation as a tax tool, consult with a qualified tax attorney.

Another major benefit to an offshore corporation is added liability protection. Many of the countries that offer tax incentives to foreign corporations have very rigorous liability protections that can serve a business well. In addition to these laws, there is the added complication of suing a foreign company.

Of course, a corporation that is established overseas will have need of credit and deposit accounts, and this will necessitate the establishment of banking relationships in any of the countries where the business will operate.

Currency Diversification

There are many currencies in the world and there are even more reasons why you might have a need to own or bank in a specific currency. Perhaps you have business dealings in a foreign country, and for convenience, wish to carry out financial transactions in that currency. Perhaps you own a summer home in Spain and wish to have Euros on hand to take care of the routine bills that this house generates. Perhaps you are the sort of person that does not believe in having "all of your eggs in one basket" and choose to keep time deposits in several major currencies to prevent the erosion of your money's purchasing power. A fall in one nation's or economic block's currency, may be balanced by the rise of another's.

It does not matter why you choose to make deposits or carry out banking business in multiple currencies. However, banking on an international level can be a way to accomplish this goal.

One of the easiest ways to own foreign currency is to simply open a bank account in one of the countries that uses that currency. This can often be accomplished through the mail with little inconvenience and almost no expense. Additionally, many banks that cater to customers on an international level are aware that their clients may have need of multiple currencies and will allow you to open accounts in many of the major world currencies. Even beyond the ability to open accounts that are denominated in any one of the world's major currencies, some banks go so far as to offer accounts that can hold multiple currencies at a single time all for your convenience. These accounts are ideal for travelers and other worldly individuals, and will be discussed in Chapter 3.

Currency Weakness

Currencies rise and fall in value based on a number of factors and can change dramatically over time. For example, the rate of growth of an economy can dramatically affect the value of a currency. As an economy slows down, less of that nation's currency is needed by the world to buy its goods and services, this increases the supply of the currency and as we all know, when supply goes up, price goes down.

Additionally, the national debt of a country can cause a sharp change in value of a nation's currency. For example, if there is concern that a nation's government can no longer continue to meet the interest obligations of its debt, the currency can plummet in value and become almost worthless.

On the reverse side of things, if a government has been extremely responsible with, for example, new found oil revenues, a countries currency can become much more sought in the world and can rise in value. The same can occur if a country has had traditionally low inflation and prudent monetary policies.

However, there are times in the past (in the future as well, we can all be sure) that a country loses control of the value of its money. When this happens, a phenomenon known as "hyperinflation" can occur. This is when the value of money plummets and ever increasingly large amount of the currency is needed to purchase even the basics. This happened in Germany in 1918, after World War I, when the economic underpinning of the German Mark collapsed amid the destruction of German industry. At points, the turmoil was so bad that wheel barrows of cash were needed to even buy a simple loaf of bread. A simple postage stamp at one point cost 5,000,000 Marks!

More recently, this type of occurrence has been seen in many parts of the developing world. The situation is not always as severe as in Germany in 1918, but can be devastating and leave people with no faith in the local currency. At times like this, people often give up on their own country's money and flock to the safety of other established currencies that are perceived as stable. This is easily done by opening an account in a foreign country that uses that currency.

Banking Insolvency

When a currency collapses, the banking system associated with that currency also faces great peril. Banks fail and are unable to make loans or even cover deposits. This can cause a run on banks like the kind that occurred in the United States in 1929 and in Argentina in 2001. Banking system can also become inherently unstable because of poor business practices like the Savings and Loan Crisis, in the United States in the 1980's. This crisis alone led to the failure of over 700 banks. When systems become unstable, citizens who can often move money to other countries whose systems are perceived as more stable, and by extension more safe. All over the developing world, it is common for the wealthy to bank in countries that are more developed.

In the United States, the FDIC is there to protect a bank's customers in the event of a bank failure, as it did during the Savings and Loan Crisis. Other developed nations have similar protections in place through either government backed insurance corporations or private bank insurance. For example, the Japanese banking system instituted the Deposit Insurance Corporation of Japan in 1971. The role of this semi-government agency is very similar to the U.S. FDIC.

However, in many parts of the world deposit insurance and government guarantees are weak is they exist at all. This can result in the loss of deposits in the even of a bank failure. This is especially common in the developing world.

This fact is an exceptionally good reason to consider offshore banking. If you are uncertain of the protection offered by your country's deposit compensation scheme or do not completely trust the state of your nation's banking system, moving some of your money to another more stable country can help to reduce the risk. In the event of a bank collapse in one country, there is still the possibility that the other country's system is continuing business as usual.

Second Chance Banking

Credit reporting has spread beyond simply whether or not you pay your bills on time. In recent decades, credit bureaus have been set up to help banks determine whether or not you are a risk based on your past conduct with previous banks. If, in the past, you have overdrawn accounts, bounced checks, or had accounts closed for one reason or another, you may not be able to open accounts in the future.

If you have gotten your act together and are still cleaning up the mess from your past, you may still not be able to open a bank account. However, this can present a real challenge to someone living in the modern world. Without a debit card or a bank account, you cannot purchase items online or receive direct payroll deposits. If you travel abroad, you would have the need to carry cash or inconvenient traveler's checks. You also have nowhere safe to put your money and can suffer from theft. This can be an intolerable situation.

One possible means to avoid these headaches is to open a foreign bank account. If you receive lots of electronic deposits, these accounts may work just as well as a domestic account. Also, these accounts, provided you conduct proper due diligence, can provide you with a safe place to store your money. With an ATM or debit card you can pay for goods and services as needed and withdraw cash when it is convenient to you.

A foreign bank account should only be used as a fresh start, not as a way to avoid cleaning up your problems at home. This means that if there are any debts that are still unresolved, you should take care of these first! However, given that everything is resolved, and only a poor track record prevents you from opening an account, foreign banks can offer a convenient alternative to life without a bank account. That is, until you can find a domestic bank that will deal with you.

Conclusion

This chapter discussed many different reasons that offshore banking may be a valid option for you to consider, when managing your finances. The following chapters will remove much of the veil of secrecy, as well as the romantic mystique, from the concept of international banking. You will learn how you can open bank accounts in many various countries around the world and the specifics that these countries offer, as well as useful information such as various world currencies, international banking products, and how to conduct due diligence to protect yourself.

2
Due Diligence

It cannot be stated enough, that moving your money beyond your home country's borders can increase the risk that you will lose your deposit. How much the risk increases depends greatly on where you choose to place your money. Moving money to well developed nations may not increase the risk to your deposits; it may even lower it in some cases. For example, Swiss banks are often considered, by some, to be among the best capitalized and most stable in the world.

However, if you choose to move money to developing nations around the world, an increase in risk will accompany the increase in interest that you will receive. If you choose to convert your money from a domestic currency to that of the developing nation's, there are even more risks that you must understand.

Additionally, moving money abroad can add extra reporting requirements, concerning taxes. Failing to comply with these laws can even make banking offshore a crime.

The past few paragraphs may paint a dark view of offshore banking. They are simply intended to make you aware that moving money across international boundaries can add risks and responsibilities that do not exist in domestic banking situations. To deal with these risks, you must have a thorough and comprehensive understanding of the economy of the country you bank in, the stability of the bank where you place your funds, the regulatory and oversight bodies that manage the countries banking system, any depositor compensation schemes or government bank guarantees that are in place, and any extra responsibilities placed on you by your domestic tax agency.

This requires detailed, country specific, research to protect yourself and the funds placed into foreign banks. In the world of business, this is known as **due diligence**.

The regulatory offices and the central banks of the country where funds are to be placed are a great place to begin your research. These websites offer many detailed reports concerning the health of that country's banking systems as well as information on bank failures should any have occurred. You should visit these sites and digest all of the information before one penny moves abroad. This book, on its own is not sufficient to base serious financial decisions on. This book is only intended as a broad guide to international and offshore banking. One's research and understanding of the bank where funds are to be deposited, as well as the advice of a qualified attorney are what serious financial decisions should be based upon. Always remember that, if your due diligence is poor, deposits can be lost forever to scams, fraud and even bank failures.

Keep Up With Current Affairs

Events in the world of banking and finance move quickly and can happen anytime of day, 365 days a year. Banks collapse, or are nationalized, laws change, investors can lose confidence, governments can be overthrown, countries invaded, volcanoes erupt, currencies devalued, and stock markets can move up or down wildly. This is more true than ever as the world banking crisis that began in 2008 continues to unfold.

If you choose to move money abroad, you need to make a commitment to keep yourself informed about the goings on of the country you move your money to and the world financial system as a whole. Never, under any circumstances, move money abroad and forget that it exists, trusting to chance that everything will be fine. There is always a chance that it will not. Take for example, the collapse of the banking system of Iceland. This came about unexpectedly, and has cost many Icelanders, as well as foreign depositors and investors billions of dollars.

Fortunately, in the age in which we live, information has never been easier to obtain. News organizations around the world churn out information every minute of the day for the consumption of the masses. Start with a familiar and reputable news source and begin to read it everyday. Once you do this, you will have a greater understanding of the world around you and will be much more able to make informed and wise decisions regarding your money.

Verify Tax Agency Reporting Rules

Depending on the tax laws of your home country, you may be required to submit a report declaring that you are in control of a foreign bank account. This is definitely true in the United States.

In the United States, as of this writing, you are required to submit, to the IRS, what is known as a "Report of Foreign Bank and Financial Account" or FBAR (IRS Form TD F 90-22.1 http://www.irs.gov/pub/irs-pdf/f90221.pdf). The FBAR is used by the IRS because foreign banks, unlike their domestic equivalents, will not necessarily report the existence of your account or any income deriving from it. For more information on IRS Foreign Bank reporting rules, visit the IRS website at http://www.irs.gov/businesses/small/article/0,,id=148849,00.html. You should also consult with your own personal qualified tax attorney. Failure to report a foreign bank account can have severe civil penalties and may even result in criminal charges.

If you do not live in the United States, consult your nation's tax agency for the most current and relevant information concerning foreign account reporting.

Lawyers & Legal Advice

At this point, you may be detecting a theme in the cautions that are in this text. You must do your homework before moving any money outside of your home country to properly understand the risks that will exist to that deposit. Also, again, keep in mind that there are always risks to your deposits in banks. Banks can fail and it may take time to recoup you deposits. This risk can and does happen.

Beyond doing your homework, it is strongly recommended that you consult a licensed attorney before moving any money abroad. An attorney's advice can be invaluable in matters such as this, and should be looked on as an investment, not a cost. They can advise you on matters of legality as well as tax implications from your overseas banking activity in relation to the current tax laws. Lawyers are also an excellent source of information concerning the previous section, account reporting.

Know Your Bankers

In international banking, banks often employ a protocol known as "Know Your Customer". This is an anti-money laundering procedure whereby the bank learns who you are and verifies your identity. This is the reason that you will be asked the purpose of the account, your profession and the source of the funds that you wish to place on deposit. The more information that a bank gathers, there is less possibility of their being used for criminal activity.

It is not a bad idea to turn this on the banks themselves. By this, it is meant, learn everything you can about the bank that you wish to do business with. Learn about the corporate structure and ownership. Many banks operating from offshore jurisdictions are wholly owned subsidiaries of very large and very well known banks from around the world.

If the bank is a publicly traded company, learn about their balance sheet. Is the bank profitable? How much money does the bank have in reserve? Have they had business problems in the recent past? What has been the recent history of their stock price?

The more you know about the bank that you want to do business with, the more certain you can be of both their legitimacy and their reliability.

Watch Out For Scams

Any work of this kind would be completely remiss if there was not a section warning about all the scams that are out there. Offshore banking, through its very nature is somewhat mysterious. Mystery is attached to the accounts, and sometimes the banks themselves. Many of the international banking centers are in remote parts of the world and in countries that many people are not familiar with. This creates an opportunity for the enterprising conman, to cheat people out of their hard earned money.

This can take many forms, but in the modern day the most common vehicle for scams of this type is the internet. There are many websites out there, purporting to be from attorneys and banking professionals. Many of these sites say that they will open accounts for you and set up everything, of course for a fee. These, are completely unnecessary, of course. Any bank that is worth your time will be happy to conduct business with you on a one-on-one basis. There is never any need for an agent simply for opening a bank account. There is a possibility that you will require an attorney for something as complicated as setting up an offshore business corporation, but that is beyond the scope of this book.

Additionally, and this is sad to say, there also exists the possibility of scam artists, representing themselves as an international bank. As a result of this, you need to be completely certain about the bona fides of any bank that you plan to conduct business with before you send the money. The best place to verify a bank's legitimacy is with the bank regulators or the central bank in Chapter 5. The bank regulator or central bank is listed in the country section for every country profiled in this book. For more information, refer to the country section.

Scams can take many different forms. They are constantly evolving and changing. Criminals and con-artists are clever people and will always come up with a new way to separate you from your money. Always be on your guard and protect your money. Remember, if it sounds too good to be true, it probably is.

Bank Regulators & Consumer Warnings

Once you have decided to open an account in a foreign country, it is always a good idea to pay a visit to the website of that country's bank regulators. The current bank regulators (these are subject to change periodically) are listed for every country presented in Chapter 5. These websites are an absolute wealth of information about a country's banking industry, the banks themselves, current events, and most relevant to this chapter; consumer warnings.

Consumer warnings are issued by bank regulators when there is a risk that consumers need to be aware of. This can take many forms. One possibility is an organization or business that is claiming something that they are not or a relationship that does not exist. An example of this would be a company fraudulently claiming to be located on the Isle of Man when they are not. Another possibility would be a business that is claiming to be licensed to perform services that in reality, they are not.

Other times, bank regulators issue consumer warning in regards to problems at a financial institution, such as a bank failure. Unfortunately, this has become more common as the world has been gripped by a global banking crisis. Changes to a country's depositor compensation plan are also often announced in the form of a consumer warning.

Whenever you decide to establish a financial relationship in a foreign country, you should read all of the current consumer warnings. The purpose of this is two fold. First, by reading all of these warnings, you will update yourself on the current state of affairs in that country's banking system. You will know if any banks have failed and why, or if there have been any other recent problems or changes. Secondly, you will be up to date on any known scams and frauds surrounding that banking system. This will make you much better prepared to avoid being a victim of any sort of fraud. The more information you have in situations like this, the better prepared you are.

Independently Verify Everything

This book teaches you the basics set of information and skill that you will need to open accounts in foreign countries. However, it is possible that no section of this book is more important than this one.

When you are moving money around the globe and giving it to institutions that you have never seen, don't take any information as fact. In every case, if information is to be relied on, it should be independently verified first. Again, don't take anything as fact (this includes all of the material in this book). For example, if a bank claims to be licensed to operate in a foreign jurisdiction, verify this with that country's bank regulators.

If you independently verify information, you will be much less likely to be taken advantage of and cheated out of your money. In the situation of a fraud occurring across international boundaries, there is little to no chance of you recovering your money.

Think About Starting Small

When just starting any relationship, there is a tendency to want to dive right in. With offshore banking, this could be an unnecessary risk or even a costly mistake.

Say for example, you have $10,000 USD that you would like to move offshore for one reason or another. You have located a bank in a jurisdiction that will serve you well and wish to open an account. The bank only requires $1,000 USD to open the account. Consider sending just the initial $1,000 and see how things proceed. If you are happy with the service you receive and become comfortable with the bank, there is no reason that you cannot send the remaining $9,000 later. However, if you find that the services of the bank are not suitable to you or in a worst case scenario that you have been defrauded out of your money, you have limited your losses.

This applies to traveling abroad too. You can always open your account with the minimum required amount and transfer more money in once you are in the foreign country. You could even deposit any cash that you have brought with you, in person, in a branch of the bank.

Country Credit Information and Economic Stability

There is no such thing as a 100% safe place to put your money. There is always some risk that you will lose value. This is a fact that any savvy investor will have to come to grips with at some point. You can place your cash under your mattress, but your house can always burn down. The government or corporation that issues your bonds may default, although the risk is lower than many other options. Even gold and oil prices have been all over the map in recent years. Before you ever place one penny of your money in a foreign institution, you need to understand and plan for the management of the increased risk you are taking. Many of the banks that cater to international clients are located in developing economic regions that may, at some point, suffer from economic recession, currency fluctuation and even bank failures. These countries, in some cases, may even suffer a coup or war. These are all situations that can cause deposited funds to evaporate almost instantly. Even if there are depositor compensation schemes and government guarantees in place, these are only as good as the central banks and governments that issue them.

No one, repeat no one, should consider moving money into a foreign country until they have researched and understand the fundamental qualities and inherent risks of a particular country's economy and banking system, as well as the stability of the government of that country. **Always remember, placing funds into an unstable economic political situation can result in the partial or complete loss of all deposited assets.** This is not meant to scare anyone, many foreign countries have a great deal to offer in terms of financial services, but is simply meant to underscore the importance of due diligence when moving money abroad.

A great place to start with your due diligence is the bank regulatory agencies that are listed for all of the countries listed in this book. (Please note inclusion in this book is by no means an endorsement of that country as an investment destination, but is provided solely for informational purposes.) These websites contain a wealth of information about their country's banking system, including deposited funds, bank failures, regulatory procedures and solvency guarantees, as well as risk analysis. Before opening any accounts, you should thoroughly research these sites. Listed central bank websites also contain vast amounts of up to date information for your perusal. These websites offer information about interest rates, national debt, bond offerings and monetary policy.

Beyond, the information provided through the websites of bank regulators and central banks, you should also investigate the credit ratings of the countries themselves. These ratings are provided by independent firms such as Standard & Poor's (www.standardandpoors.com) and Moody's (www.moodys.com). These are only examples and there other firms that offer similar risk management information. You can often find these ratings free of charge using the Internet. Before making any decisions, you should consult these figures and understand what they mean. <u>Remember, only your money is at risk.</u>

Federal Deposit Insurance Corporation

In 1933 when the United States was recovering from the worst of the Great Depression, an Act of Congress created the Federal Deposit Insurance Corporation or FDIC. One of the largest contributing factors to the Great Depression was people were afraid that banks would fail and take their life saving's with them into bankruptcy.

Congress through the creation of the FDIC, hoped to reassure the American people that their deposits in banks were safe and they would receive their money even in the event of a bank failure. The FDIC achieved this purpose by insuring all deposits in qualified accounts such as savings and checking accounts. Currently, in the United States, each <u>depositor</u>, not account, at an FDIC insured bank (there are some that are not) is insured for at least $100,000. This was temporarily raised to $250,000 until the end of 2009. This insurance is backed by all the financial resources of the United States Government. This again only applies to specific account types but is rock solid protection that has served Americans well through the Great Depression and the Savings and Loan Crisis. It is very valuable protection that should be appreciated and understood.

All of the banking relationships that are discussed in this book are **not FDIC insured**. This means that in the event of a bank failure, the United States government through the FDIC will have no responsibility whatsoever to replace lost funds. **You can loose money in the event of an international bank failure.** Now, many of the foreign countries that have offshore banking industries have similar protection systems. These will be detailed in Chapter 5. However, it should be crystal clear that the United States Government will offer no help at all.

Foreign Depositor Compensation Plans

In the United States, as was stated, depositors are protected by the FDIC. However many countries around the world have not developed these programs. Small nations in the developing world that have built international banking centers often do not have compensation programs. These can require substantial monetary guarantees that these small governments are not in a position to make. Instead, these countries tend to put in place, as depositor protections, rigorous supervision and oversight programs. Another method of protection is to only permit the largest and most established banks to operate from a jurisdiction.

Many developed nations, do however, offer depositor compensation plans. In 2008, the governments of Germany, Ireland and Great Britain all guaranteed the deposits in their banks to some extent. These decisions were in response to a crisis in liquidity, but are examples of non-FDIC depositor protections. Even before this, many developed nations, including all EU member states, had plans in place.

If a country that is profiled in this book has a depositor compensation plan, it will be mentioned in the profile along with where you can find the most current details of the plan.

Inflation Concerns

Inflation is another measure of a country's financial health, which you should understand. Inflation is the rise in prices annually, and in consequence the decrease in the purchasing power of that countries currency. Inflation is a natural part of a capitalist economy and can not be completely eliminated according to classical economics. However, keeping the inflation rate of a country low is one of the essential jobs of any central bank. The CIA maintains a list of global inflation rates that can be found at https://www.cia.gov/library/publications/the-world-factbook/fields/2092.html.

Inflation can be caused by many factors and is the subject of constant debate among economists. Several causes of inflation are the amount of money in circulation, the rate of unemployment and the demand for goods. In the developed world, inflation is generally low (less than 5% or so); however, in countries whose economies are in a state of collapse, inflation can hit astronomical numbers. Argentina experienced a monthly inflation rate of 10.4% in 2002 and more recently, Zimbabwe experienced a staggering inflation rate of 231,000,000% (that is not a typo, 231 million percent) as recently as 2008.

You should also be aware that currencies can experience sudden and dramatic inflation. This is one of the reasons that you may be offered a higher rate of interest for accounts denominated in a local currency versus on denominated in a major world currency. Before making any decisions of this nature, consult your own financial planner as well as an attorney. Additionally, you should conduct research into the current inflation rates and risks about currency you are considering purchasing.

Notes On The Banking Crisis

Beginning in late 2008 and continuing to the present (as of the writing of this book) many large banks across the globe have failed. In addition, many governments have had to step into the affairs of banks based in their countries and issue large amounts of cash and credit to keep consumer credit and lending flowing. Even beyond that, many jurisdictions have implemented depositor compensation schemes for the first time, as well as blanket guarantees for deposits in their banks. In the case of Iceland, the whole banking systems has collapsed. This is an extraordinary time for the banking industry.

This is not to say that the world banking system is in jeopardy. Additionally, this is not to say that there are not needs and benefits to moving your money across international boundaries. You are the best person, along with a qualified attorney, to decide what is best for your personal situation. However, this crisis should make anyone take pause and carefully study the potential risks of international banking. You need to know the absolute current information about the banking system in the country in which you are involved. The bank regulators of a country are one of the best resources, and these are listed in the World Banking Almanac in Chapter 5. Additionally, study recent media articles and know what is going on. Again, you only have your money to lose if you make a bad decision.

International Banking Centers & The Global Community

Unfortunately, there are criminals and terrorists that try to take advantage of the world financial system to hide their ill-gotten gains or to finance violence. This is a sad fact of life.

Fortunately for the honest investor the global community has worked hard in the last few decades to make money laundering, and more recently terrorist financing, much harder.

The main engine driving this fight is the Financial Action Task Force on Money Laundering (FATF, www.fatf-gafi.org), which is an administrative arm of the Organization for Economic Co-operation and Development (OECD, www.oecd.org). The FATF is a 32 member nation group that was founded with the express purpose of closing loopholes in offshore banking systems that were permissive to money laundering.

The 32 members of the FATF represent most of the countries of the developed world and account for the majority of economic activity in the whole world. This group monitors banking systems around the world and maintains a set of standards that reputable banking centers must comply with to avoid sanction. If a country or territory, in the opinion of the FATF, does not comply with the established rules, the country can be designated as a Non-cooperative Country or Territory, or NCCT. This is essentially a blacklist of world banking systems, and can be devastating to the listed country's reputation. If a country is placed on this list, they may continue to conduct international business; however, other banks must thoroughly examine and analyze any transactions. This places a large burden of cost and time on the receiving bank. Many will simply refuse to do business with banks in countries on the list of NCCTs.

The first list of NCCT countries was published in 2000 and included 23 countries. Since then, all of the countries that were listed have implemented satisfactory policies and laws to be removed from the list. Most recently, under pressure from the OECD and the threat of an NCCT listing, Switzerland amended its bank secrecy laws allow information sharing in the event of a criminal investigation. If a country in Chapter 5 was listed on the NCCT in 2001 or has had recent dealing with the OECD, this will be discussed.

The Egmont Group (www.egmontgroup.org) is another group that works to protect the international banking system from abuse and criminal activity. This informal international organization is composed of more than one hundred financial intelligence units (FIUs) from around the world. These units work to analyze bank transactions, searching for evidence of criminal behavior. If any illegal activity is found, the FIU works in concert with law enforcement to bring the guilty to justice.

The Egmont Group is named after the Belgian palace in Brussels where the first international conference of the group took place in 1995. Since the initial meeting, this group has continued to gain new members as well as meet regularly to stay abreast of developments in money laundering activities.

Conclusion

Understanding that there is risk associated with moving your money around the world is one of the most important lessons that this book teaches. You alone are responsible for protecting your money. This can only be done by conducting due diligence and research, and making informed, educated decisions (in cooperation with a qualified attorney), that are relevant to your personal situation.

3 Offshore Banking Basics

This chapter will explore some basic concepts that you will need to understand before banking internationally. Some basic terms regarding international and offshore banking will be defined. This chapter also explores the account types that you will encounter when attempting to open accounts abroad, as well as the major currencies used by banks worldwide. All of this information will be absolutely necessary before you open an account.

Offshore Banking Defined

There is a matter of semantics that should be cleared up at this point. This is the term "offshore banking".

The term offshore banking is one that stirs up all kinds of all kinds of connotations. Often, people will think of luxury and privilege. These perceptions can arise from any number of origins. Most commonly, these types of ideas surrounding offshore banking come from people not understanding the needs of international banking relationships or the benefits of these relationships. Bank secrecy laws, while beneficial, only help to increase this misunderstanding. In the past unscrupulous people have attempted to hide their money in offshore banks, hoping these laws would hide the profits of their crimes or shield them from legitimate taxation.

These ideas of luxury and criminal abuse of the system can make offshore banking misunderstood. However, from reading the Chapter 1, you are aware that there are many very real and prudent reasons for a person to move some of their assets abroad. Also, as the world continues to become more integrated more people will realize the benefits of banking internationally. This book is aimed at those people.

Throughout this work, the term "offshore banking" will only refer to the practice of utilizing the services of banks in foreign countries for legitimate purposes, not the practice of hiding money to avoid taxes.

This term will also be used synonymously with the term "international banking".

The Two Types Of International Banks

There are two types of international banks that will be discussed in this book. These bank types should be thought of as "foreign" banks and "offshore" banks.

Foreign banks are simply commercial banks that operate in a foreign country. They are just like the banks whose services you would seek if you wanted to open a checking account in your home country. They open checking accounts, certificates of deposit and issue loans. Loans and fees make up the majority of the bank's revenue.

Seeking the services of a foreign bank could be appropriate if you would like to have an account denominated in the currency of a particular country, wish to have access to a local bank while you are traveling or wish to make use of a foreign bank for convenience in business. For example, if you wanted to open a Euro account, you could seek the services of a commercial bank in Malta, Germany or France.

Another reason to open a foreign bank account would be if you are planning to live in a foreign country for an extended period of time. For example, if you are going to live in Finland for a while and wish to be able to walk into a local bank for face to face service, you will need to seek the services of a foreign bank located in Finland.

Offshore banks are different. Offshore banks, generally speaking, operate from jurisdictions that have specifically tailored tax policies, government regulations and privacy laws that make them a desirable locale for wealthy individuals to bank from. Most of the time, the customers of these banks do not live in the country where their bank operates. In fact, many traditional offshore jurisdictions have specific offshore banking licenses that forbid these banks to carry out business with local citizens. This type of bank is in the business of carrying out financial transactions and wealth management only. As a general rule, they do not offer consumer loans or credit products. The majority of these bank's revenues are made up of fees and management services.

Offshore bank services are appropriate for seeking lower taxes (working with an attorney), liability protection, wealth management, investment services, and privacy regarding finances, etc. For example, many lottery winners complain about the fame and attention that winning the lottery gives them. This has become such a problem, that many states have passed laws that permit the winners of the lottery to remain anonymous. If you won the lottery and wished to continue your life without anyone learning about your new immense wealth, an offshore bank account in a low tax country could be an excellent place to deposit your funds, providing of course you observe all relevant tax laws.

How Much Money Is Necessary?

In decades past, international banking was the sole province of the wealthy. Contacting banks, and traveling to foreign locales required lots of money. Even finding some of the banks (some have preferred to keep low profiles) and communicating via mail could be a very time consuming process. All of this has changed.

Today, many international banks understand that the products and services that they offer may be of use to smaller net worth individuals. Many middle class individuals might be interested in diversifying their investment portfolios with high interest, foreign bank CDs or in keeping their savings in more than one currency. Also, small business owners may have just as much incentive to take advantage of the asset protection services offered by foreign jurisdictions as do transnational corporations. As such, one can find a bank to suit just about any sized deposit, or any sought after service.

You will be required to transfer some money, however, and minimums range quite a bit. The bare minimum that you must be prepared to move into an offshore bank is $1,000 USD or the equivalent in one of the other major currencies. However, $50,000-$100,000 USD or the equivalent another major currency is a fairly standard amount to be required for opening a bank account in an international offshore banking center. As a general rule, Caribbean banks look for smaller minimum account opening deposits than their European counterparts.

These requirements are in place for several reasons. Firstly, opening bank accounts across international boundaries is expensive. There is the time of the banking professionals as well as postage that needs to be considered. Secondly, offshore banks are not in the business of providing accounts for daily use. Most of the banks in international banking centers are in the business of long time asset management and wealth development. If you are planning to pay your monthly bills out of this account, you would be better off opening an account at your local hometown bank. Few, if any, of these banks will provide you with an ATM card. The money that is to be deposited into an offshore bank should generally be money that is to be left alone and permitted to grow undisturbed. Requiring a large initial deposit ensures the bank that you are an individual who has enough capital to need their services.

However, if you do wish to open an account in a foreign country for daily access and use, say while you are traveling aboard, the story is entirely different. These banks are used to dealing with average customers who range the spectrum of net worth. In the United States it is common to require about $100 USD to open an account. This translates fairly well to commercial banks operating in countries around the world. In Canada, accounts can be opened with a similar amount. In some parts of the Caribbean, however, accounts can be opened for less than $20 USD.

International Banking Is Not Always Free

Commercial banks that simply operate in a foreign country will not usually charge you account opening fees. However, this is not true of accounts in traditional offshore jurisdictions. These banks, and indirectly the governments of these areas, can and will charge fees to open accounts. In addition, you will often be required to pay annual account maintenance fees. These fees vary depending on the service that is being sought. Establishing a simple bank account in an offshore jurisdiction is fairly straight forward and the fee for such an account is usually several hundred U.S. Dollars, plus an annual account maintenance fee. However, more complicated processes such as establishing offshore trusts and accounts to support such an entity can easily cost tens of thousands of U.S. Dollars. Additionally, you can plan on an annual account maintenance fee of at least $1,000 USD as well.

These fees are relative and should be carefully considered before you open your account. For example, storing $10,000 in an account that costs $300 to open and $100 per year after that may seem a tad expensive. It is. You are essentially paying a 4% fee the first year that the account is open, simply to park your money. On the other hand, storing $1,000,000 in the same account is only a .04% fee. This small percentage, when compared with the investment returns and privacy that many of these banks offer, can be well worth it.

It is not difficult to discover the fee structure that a prospective bank will charge. The disclosure of these fee structures is mandated by law and will be provided to you along with any other account opening documents such as applications and source disclosures. If for some bizarre reason, these fees are not volunteered with your initial paperwork, you must ask for a written fee structure. If the information is still not forthcoming, look elsewhere for your financial service needs. Never establish a relationship with a bank without a thorough understanding of their fee structure.

Small States & International Banking

Many international banking centers are located in geographically small places. Islands in the Caribbean such as The Turks and Caicos Islands or The Cayman Islands are very small. The same can be said of the islands in the Pacific Ocean. International offshore banking centers in Europe are no different. Andorra, The Isle of Man, Guernsey, Jersey and Liechtenstein, although not all islands, are also very small countries. The populations of these areas are fractions of what would be called small cities in many places around the world.

You may ask yourself, if these countries are so small in size and population, why have they become such beacons of international finance? To fully appreciate why international banking centers have developed in these areas, you must stop and consider the economic situations of these areas.

These countries, like all others in the world wish to become fully integrated, respected members of the community of nations and ensure the peace and prosperity of their citizenry. Economic status is definitely a huge boost to such aspirations. Money is needed to fund public works and low unemployment is a goal of every government. Unfortunately, most of the countries where international banking centers have developed are poor in natural resources. Countries such as the Bahamas do not have much arable land, there is no oil in Bermuda, and the Isle of Man lacks sparkling white sand beaches. While the populations in these areas are educated and technically proficient, many of these areas are also geographically isolated. Andorra and Liechtenstein do not have ports from which to ship finished manufactured products to foreign customers overseas.

International banking offers a solution to all these problems. International banking brings in large amounts of deposits that can in turn be loaned to stimulate the economy, and generates revenue in the form of government fees. Once banks move into an area, they need people to work for them. This creates the jobs needed by an educated, but isolated workforce. Also, with the development of modern communication infrastructures, geographic isolation ceases to be a problem. It is as easy wire money to Europe or Asia as quickly as you can wire it across town.

International Banking Products & Services

Before you decide what services offered by international banks might be right for you, you need to know a little about the services that these banks will offer you. In the following pages, you will find a brief description of the most common services that will be available to you. There may be subtle variations in these products across countries and economic regions, and it is very possible that not all of these services will be available to you. This is entirely dependent on the current laws and bank policies in place once you contact a particular bank. Additionally, as was discussed a few pages ago, the services of international banks is not always free and there may be fees associated with some if not all of these services.

Deposit Accounts

Deposit accounts will be offered by almost every international and foreign bank you contact. These accounts offer the same services that you are used to with domestic checking and savings accounts. In a nutshell, you place your funds in a bank. The bank then holds the funds, and may pay you interest. Usually this interest rate will be fairly low in comparison to term deposits. Names for these accounts vary, but they will usually be called checking, savings or current accounts.

Which types of deposit accounts will be available to you will depend on the laws of the country where you wish to establish an account. If the country in question is an established offshore banking center, it is likely; all account types will be available to you.

If however, you choose to bank in a foreign country that is not an established international banking center, your options will be more limited. If you are not permitted to earn interest, as will be the case in many developed nations (you cannot pay tax as a nonresident, so you cannot earn interest that would need to be taxed), you will be limited to accounts that are not paid interest. If you are not allowed to be issued credit as a non-resident, you will not be permitted to have a debit card. Many countries around the world take the privilege of check writing very seriously and will not permit their banks to open a checking account for non-residents.

ATM & Debit Cards

For most people in the United States, their debit card is also their ATM card. This is true abroad as well. However, there may be restrictions on debit cards for a non-resident alien.

It is possible for a debit card user to overdraw their account as the result of their activity. If the bank permits a transaction to go through which overdraws the account, they pay the merchant and then collect the necessary funds from the customer. This is essentially the issuance of credit. Issuance of credit to a foreign citizen is restricted by law in many countries.

While restrictions do exist on debit cards, ATM cards are frequently issued to foreign citizens. Since these cards are simply used to access your funds, this eliminates the potential issuance of credit. You will be issued a card as well as a PIN number. This can often be done through the mail. However, to change a PIN you will need to present yourself at a branch. This can be a problem if the closest branch is on a different continent, so make sure to keep track of your documents.

You will be able to use your ATM card to access funds if you wish. However, recall that there will not be a local branch or ATM in your home country, so if you do use an ATM, you will most likely be charged a fee by the foreign bank and the bank whose ATM you used.

This can make frequent withdrawals from a foreign bank through an ATM an expensive proposition and inappropriate for everyday use.

Multiple Currency Accounts

With ever-increasing global trade and ease of travel, many people are using multiple currencies in their lives. This is especially true in European countries such as Great Britain and Switzerland who border countries that use the Euro. These countries share long demilitarized borders and friendly relations that make travel and business very attractive.

Converting between various international currencies can sometimes be inconvenient and costly. It could be that exchange rates have shifted and the bearer will lose purchasing power by exchanging one currency for another. It could also be that future trips or business will require one currency instead of another and the bearer wishes to avoid exchange fees. Either way, they wish to continue to hold all of their currency in their current form.

To respond to the needs of their customers, many international banks are beginning to offer multiple currency accounts. These accounts, instead of being limited to single currency, can take deposits and hold most of the six major world currencies (U.S. Dollars, Euros, Swiss Francs, Canadian Dollars, Pounds Sterling and Japanese Yen). Some British banks will also offer to take on deposit and hold Australian and New Zealand Dollars as well.

If your personal financial situation necessitates holding multiple currencies, or you wish to diversify your holdings with the addition of international currencies, this type of account may be of interest to you.

Term Deposit Accounts

Term deposits, also often called "Certificates of Deposit" or simply "CDs" are a very common and popular banking product offered by banks across the globe.

A term deposit is simply this. You take some of your capital and tell a bank that you will place it on deposit in the bank for a certain amount of time that you will guarantee. For example, you place $10,000 USD in a bank for a guaranteed period of 12 months. This is good for the bank. They need to maintain a certain ratio between deposits and loans and they can now count on your $10,000 for the next twelve months. The bank can also loan out the money and make interest on it.

Now there is a cost to you in terms of the availability of the $10,000. While you still own the money, you cannot access it for the next twelve months without incurring a penalty. To compensate you for this inconvenience, the bank will pay you a higher rate of interest than in an account that allows you to withdraw your money as you see fit. This is what makes it a more attractive and popular investment vehicle than a deposit account. You get a higher rate of return, for money that you do not wish to lock up in stocks or bonds, that is relatively safe, than you would if it were simply kept as cash.

Additionally, term deposits are often protected by a country's deposit compensation scheme. This of course, varies between countries and should be verified before putting any funds on deposit.

Term deposits can be denominated in any currency that a bank chooses to conduct business. Additionally terms for CDs range from anywhere from three months to ten years.

Wealth Management Services

For many of the banks that operate in international banking jurisdictions, taking deposits, and making loans are secondary business operations. For many of these banks, their primary business activity is wealth management and investment advising.

This is a service, that, if you are a high net worth individual, you would be foolish to ignore. These banks will be happy to discuss their programs with you in detail either in person or over the phone. Of course, many of the banks that offer these services will require you to place a sum somewhere between $100,000 and $250,000 under their management to take advantage of these services. Additionally, these services are not free. There are management fees and percentages of returns on investment that will be paid to the bank for their services. You should have a complete and thorough understanding of these fee structures before committing any funds to management.

Lastly, you need to have an intimate understanding of the risks underlying any investments that you may choose to participate in through foreign firms. As we have all seen from recent event, a poorly understand investment can result in massive financial losses. It is your responsibility, and yours alone, to safeguard your capital as you see fit. Never under any circumstances, take the word of an investment counselor at face value. Always do your due diligence to protect your capital and investments from loss. You should also be aware that under most circumstances, funds placed in banks for investment purposes are not insured by deposit compensation schemes and may lose value due to market fluctuations and the possibility of a bank failure. As always, for the most current and relevant information speak with a licensed attorney.

Fiduciary Deposit Services

Fiduciary deposit services are another service that is commonly offered by international banks. This makes complete sense due to the nature of fiduciary deposits.

A fiduciary deposit is a deposit made by a bank to a second bank on the behalf of their client. The bank that makes the deposit makes it in the name of the client, not on its behalf. Any interest that is paid is paid directly to the client and not the depositing bank.

Banks that offer fiduciary services, often have a much more intimate knowledge of the world banking system than, you a private citizen, would. This means that they can seek higher returns and are in a better position to manage risk. Additionally, internationally recognized banks can move money around the globe with more ease than a private individual can.

Fiduciary deposits have a number of benefits. Firstly, because of their expertise with global interest rates as well as inflation and risk, professional bank money managers may be able to better and more easily manage your money than you can. There are also potential tax advantages. This is entirely dependent on the laws of the country where the bank that makes the fiduciary deposit. For example, in Switzerland, interests from fiduciary deposits are treated as non-Swiss interest and are free from income taxation.

To take advantage of fiduciary deposits, you will often need to commit sums as large as $100,000 USD. You will also often be able to determine the length of the deposit as you would with a certificate of deposit. Lastly, plan to pay a fee for this service. Fees range between banks and between countries, so it is wise to do some shopping around before committing any funds.

Credit Products

As a general rule, credit products will not be available to you as a foreign national. Again, this is because foreign banks may have trouble determining your credit worthiness as well as securing collateral for any loans. Additionally, the laws of the country where you choose to bank will often prevent you from receiving credit.

Deposit Boxes

In addition to traditional deposit accounts, some international banks choose to offer deposit box services. These boxes can be used to store investments of all kinds from cash, to precious metals and jewels and even works of art.

Because these boxes could be easily misused to conceal ill gotten money or even stolen works of art, these boxes are not issued lightly. Each financial institution and country will have its own requirements for issuance of these boxes. To receive a deposit box you will need to satisfy the bank's compliance department as to your legitimacy.

Precious Metal Investing

If you are in possession of large amounts of precious metals, or you wish to convert your currency into precious metals, some international banks will offer you precious metal deposit services. This is essentially when the bank takes your gold, silver, platinum or even palladium on deposit. You will receive a deposit receipt just like when you deposit cash. The metals will then be stored in the banks facilities with a high level of security. This type of banking tends to be a specialty of banks in Switzerland and Liechtenstein.

<u>Major World Currencies</u>

To carry out banking business across international boundaries, you will need to be familiar with some of the currencies in which you will be banking. There are many currencies around the world and you can really bank in any of them. However, there are eight major currencies in which the majority world financial transactions are carried out in.

Generally, foreign banks will offer accounts only in their own country's currency. However, sometimes, if two neighboring countries share strong economic ties, banks will offer accounts in both of their currencies. For example, U.S. Dollar accounts are very common in Canada. Most offshore banks will be able to offer you an account or term deposit in which your funds are held in at least several, if not all of the currencies that are listed below.

United States Dollar (USD)

The United States Dollar abbreviated "USD" and marked with the symbol "$" is the official currency of the United States of America. U.S. Dollar currency is issued by the United States Federal Reserve which is the central bank of the United States. The U.S. Dollar is one of the major currencies in the world and enjoys several special distinctions. All precious metals from silver to gold or platinum are always priced in USD, no matter where in the world the transaction takes place. Additionally, any sale or purchase of oil or oil contracts is always carried out in USD. This has led to the development of the term "petrodollars". Recently some major oil exporters have begun to voice an opinion that this should be changed with the Euro replacing the U.S. Dollar. However, Saudi Arabia, one of the largest oil exporters in the world has voiced unwavering support for the U.S. Dollar pricing. This means that this practice is likely to continue for some time.

The United States Dollar also enjoys the status of being the most widely held currency by foreign governments. Even as late as 2007, almost 60% of all foreign currency held by world governments was held in USD.

In addition to the United States, several other countries use the USD as their official currency. Countries using the dollar as official currency include Ecuador and Panama. Two British Overseas Territories, The Turks and Caicos and The British Virgin Islands also use the United States Dollar as their official currency. Many other nations in Latin America and the Caribbean have also officially pegged their currencies, at a fixed rate to the USD.

The United States Dollar has suffered compared with other international currencies in recent years due to growing deficits in the United States economy, however, the dollar is still a major world currency and accounts where funds are held in USD will be offered by most offshore banks.

Euro (EUR)

The Euro is the official currency of the European Union, a political and social alliance between member nations primarily in Western Europe. The Euro is denoted by the abbreviation "EUR" or the symbol "€". The Euro can be subdivided into one hundred cents often called "Eurocents". The Euro is a newcomer to world currencies and only began circulation in 2002. Since that time it has achieved a reputation as a stable currency and is a challenger to the supremacy of the USD. This has led many central banks to acquire large amounts of Euros for their foreign currency holdings, although the United States Dollar is still the widest held currency in the world.

The Euro is a truly international currency. This currency, alone among major world currencies, is issued by the fifteen member states that make up the Eurozone. At present, the Eurozone includes Spain, Portugal, Ireland, France, Germany, Malta, Belgium, The Netherlands, Italy, Austria, Finland, Cyprus, Luxembourg, Slovenia, and Greece.

The Euro is also the official currency of San Marino, Andorra, Monaco and Vatican City. Many of the former Soviet states of Eastern Europe have pegged their currency to the Euro in anticipation of joining the Eurozone in the near future.

Two notable exceptions to the Eurozone are the United Kingdom and Sweden. The government of the U.K. has opted against adoption of the Euro, and support for the Euro in Great Britain remains luke warm. Also, a referendum in Sweden in 2003 voted against the adoption of the Euro, and the Swedish government is not pushing the matter forward. However, Sweden is required to adopt the Euro under the terms of the EU membership, so this issue is still an evolving one.

The stability of the Euro is monitored by the European Central Bank. This bank is the central bank of the European Union and monitors and regulates the activities of the central banks of the member states of the European Union. The international banking centers of Europe, with the exceptions of Switzerland and Liechtenstein, will treat the Euro as their default currency. Fees and minimum deposits will be quoted in Euros as well.

Swiss Franc (CHF)

The Swiss Franc is the national currency of Switzerland and Liechtenstein. This currency is issued by the Swiss National Bank, and after the introduction of the Euro in France, is the only Franc currency remaining in Europe. The Swiss Franc is the fifth most popularly traded currency in the world and is abbreviated by the symbol "CHF".

While the United States Dollar and the Euro are highly sought currencies due to the needs of trade with the United States and the European Union, the Swiss Franc is primarily sought because of its stable history and the low inflation in the Swiss economy. The fact that Switzerland has not been to war in centuries only adds to this perceived stability. The Swiss Franc has also been backed by larger amounts of gold held in the Swiss National Bank, as opposed to other central banks around the world. This amount of gold has dropped in recent years but does remain comparatively high.

Many international banks will be happy to conduct business in Swiss Francs. This is not limited to banks in Switzerland and Liechtenstein, but will apply to Europe, the Caribbean, and Asia as well.

Great British Pound Sterling (GBP)

The Pound Sterling is the currency of the United Kingdom. Banknotes are issued by the Bank of England and this central bank is responsible for monetary policy that ensures the strength of the pound. Pounds sterling are represented by the "£" symbol and the currency is abbreviated "GBP". A single pound used to broken up into 20 shillings with each shilling being worth 12 pence. This system was replaced in 1971 and one pound was divisible into 100 pennies. Pennies are abbreviated with the letter "p", as in this costs "80p".

Although the British Empire is a thing of the past, the economy of Great Britain is still one of the largest in the world. This creates a requirement for foreign countries to buy pounds if they wish to deal with the British. This adds greatly to the demand for Pounds Sterling.

Great Britain is also a member of the European Union even although it has chosen not to use the Euro as its official currency. This is by special arrangement within the European Union. The debate about adopting the Euro in Britain does continue, although public opinion has been consistently against it.

Canadian Dollar (CAD)

The currency of Canada is also known as the dollar. Like the United States Dollar this monetary unit is symbolized with the symbol "$". However, the international abbreviation for the Canadian Dollar is "CAD". The Canadian Dollar is issued the Bank of Canada who oversees monetary policy in Canada as well.

The Canadian Dollar is less important as a global currency than the United States Dollar, Euro, Pound Sterling or Swiss Franc; however it is still a commonly traded currency and is held by central banks around the world as a reserve currency.

Canada's main trading partners are in North America. The United States accounts for the vast majority of Canada's foreign trade, but Canada also carries on trade with Latin America and the Caribbean. Because of the role of the United States as Canada's primary trading partner, it is the relationship between the USD and the CAD that is most closely observed. This relationship has rearranged itself a number of times during the last 50 years. There have been times when the USD was worth more than the CAD, and the opposite is equally true.

You will commonly find banks that will conduct business in Canadian dollars in the Caribbean region as well as the Isle of Man, Guernsey and Jersey. Historically, the CAD has been a relatively stable currency although inflation concerns have arisen in the past.

Japanese Yen (JPY)

The Yen is the currency of the nation of Japan and is the third most widely traded currency in the world currency markets. The yen is identified with the "¥" symbol and is abbreviated with the standard code of "JPY". The yen is the integral unit of the Japanese currency system and is not subdivided. The only coins in circulation are the ¥1, ¥5, ¥10, ¥50, ¥100, ¥500. Notes are issued in denominations of ¥1000, ¥2000, ¥5000, ¥10,000. Prices of goods are always quoted in whole yen numbers. There is no fractional yen. This is similar to the United States choosing to use only the penny as its currency. Instead of saying a soda costs $1.50 we would say that the soda costs 150 pennies.

After World War II, the yen lost most of its value and was pegged to the United States Dollar. Since 1973, the yen has been permitted to float against other world currencies.

Since the yen was permitted to float against other international currencies, there has been a steady decline in its value as opposed to other world currencies. This is in part caused by the recession that Japan experienced in the late 1980s and early 1990s as well as the Bank of Japan's extremely low interest rates when compared with the interest rates offered by other central banks around the world.

Australian Dollar (AUD)

The Australian Dollar is the official currency of Australia as well as a number of other dependent territories and independent island nations in the Southern Pacific.

The Australian Dollar is abbreviated with the letters "AUD" and is symbolized, in Australia, with the familiar dollar symbol, "$". Outside of Australia, the Australian dollar is often abbreviated with "AU$", in order to differentiate between other dollar currencies, such as Canada and The United States.

The Australian Dollar is issued by the Reserve Bank of Australia, who is responsible for the monetary policies that govern its stability. The dollar is also allowed to float against other world currencies. The

Australian dollar is a less common international currency but is still commonly accepted by deposit institutions outside of Australia, especially by former British colonies and British Overseas Territories. The Australian dollar is also a commonly held reserve currency, but in smaller amounts than the six major world currencies.

New Zealand Dollar (NZD)

The New Zealand Dollar is the official currency of the islands of New Zealand. This currency is also notable as it is an accepted currency in the international banking center of the Cook Islands, which is an independent nation in association with New Zealand.

Like the Australian Dollar, the new Zealand Dollar is symbolized with the "$" symbol. Also, like the Australian Dollar, the New Zealand Dollar is symbolized outside of New Zealand to differentiate between other dollar currencies. The commonly used symbol is "NZ$". The Reserve Bank of New Zealand is responsible for issuing and maintaining the stability of the New Zealand Dollar and does permit the currency to float in global exchanges.

Conclusion

In this chapter, we defined the scope of international banking and defined some of the key terms that will be used through the remainder of this book. Common services offered by banks around the world were also discussed. Lastly, information regarding major currencies of the world was presented. This information will be absolutely necessary to you in your understanding of international banking, and as you continue onto Chapter 4, in which the mechanics of opening international bank accounts will be explained.

4 Opening Foreign Accounts

If you have ever opened a bank account previously, you have a pretty good idea of the process of opening a foreign bank account. In a nutshell, you will need to contact the bank, either in person or through the mail, provide the bank with an application, supporting documents such as identification and make an initial deposit. The bank will review the documents and information that you provide to them, and if you are approved by the compliance department, the bank will open an account for you.

The process of opening a foreign account as opposed to opening a domestic account differs in the details. There are many small differences in the two processes. For example, when opening an account through the mail, you will need to satisfactorily prove your identity without ever setting foot in that bank's country. How do you do this? You may need to wire funds to another continent and have no idea what an IBAN is. You may need to obtain a bank reference letter from your current bank. If you, yourself, do not know what that is, you will have a hard time explaining it to your confused banker.

This chapter seeks to explain all the little differences that may present themselves while you are seeking to open a foreign bank account. The answers to the questions presented above, as well as many others, are presented in the following pages.

Finding A Bank

Finding a suitable foreign bank begins with identifying a country that offers the banking benefits that you desire. This may be location, privacy laws, currency, or any of the other benefits discussed in Chapter 1. Chapter 5 of this book will discuss many developed countries and offshore banking centers. In no way, does inclusion in this part of this book constitute an endorsement of any country. This is merely a list of countries that may offer you the services that you seek.

Once you have identified a suitable country, you should begin searching for a specific bank by visiting the website of the bank regulation agency, which is often the country's central bank. These will often provide lists of licensed banks and other deposit companies permitted to operate within that country's jurisdictions. The bank regulator of each country profiled in this book will be listed in Chapter 5 as well.

Equally important, you will often find posted warnings and updates concerning the banking system. This could be something simple such as the issuance of a new license to a new bank or an update to the country's depositor compensation scheme. There may be updates or press releases concerning recent bank failures. Very importantly, there could be information about companies that are misrepresenting themselves as permitted to operate within the jurisdiction, when in fact they are not. It is a sad fact that some people attempt to take advantage of other people's ignorance and lack of due diligence in order to cheat them. You should always check the warnings from the bank regulators as well as the licenses of any banks with those regulators as part of your due diligence effort.

Once you have read the regulator warnings, you can begin to look for a licensed bank to establish a relationship. Links to lists of banks licensed to operate in the countries in this book will also be provided. Review the website of each bank that seems to be a possibility and conduct thorough research. Find out what services they offer and decide which bank best fits your needs.

Contacting Your Choice of Bank

Once you have found a bank that fits your particular set of needs, you need to establish contact with them to request account opening information as well as to determine if their policies will permit you, as a foreign citizen to open an account. This will require you to obtain the contact information of the bank. This information is almost always available on the bank's website. Look for the link that says "Contact Us" in most cases (provided of course that the website is in English). This will provide you with email contact, phone numbers, and a branch locator in many cases.

There are two ways that you can contact the bank. The first is to contact their corporate customer service department. The other method is to directly contact a branch of the bank. If you are opting to bank in a country, whose language you do not speak, it is best to contact the corporate office. There is a much greater possibility of you finding someone who speaks your language there. However, if you contact a specific branch, especially one that you can visit personally in the near future, you are more likely to receive personalized customer service, and to find someone willing to work with your specific needs.

In the days of the Internet, email is by far the best method of contacting banks in a foreign country. Firstly, this method of communication sidesteps the inconvenience of world time zones. The recipient of the email can respond to your inquiry at their convenience, even if it is while you are asleep on the other side of the world.

Additionally, language barriers can more easily be avoided through email communication. If the person receiving the email is not completely fluent in your native language or speaks with a heavy accent, which is frequently the case, email permits the response to be written out carefully and without any distortion in meaning.

No matter how you choose to contact the bank in questions, you need to clearly explain your needs. Tell them why you wish to open an account and that you are a non-resident, foreign citizen. Ask whomever you speak with to provide you with account options and an application packet if they offer one. Make sure you enquire as to what types of documents you will need to present to the bank in order to open an account. Once you receive all of this information you are ready to proceed. If, on the other hand, the bank responds that they are unable to open an account for you, simply cross them off and proceed to the next one on your list.

Making Phone Calls Abroad

Some banks will just not conduct their business over email, which is a very convenient method for communicating across oceans and time zones. As was stated, email is also very convenient for overcoming language barriers. If the bank that wish to establish a relationship with falls among this group, you will have to resort to making phone calls the old fashioned way.

The first bit of information that someone making an international phone call must have is the phone number of the destination they wish to call. If you live within the United States or Canada, you are most likely familiar with the concept of an area code. However, if you have never had reason to call internationally or have never traveled abroad, you may be unfamiliar with country codes. This code acts just like an area code, however it tells the phone system, which country you are calling, instead of which part of a country. You most likely have already used a country code without knowing it. In the United States and Canada it is not uncommon to dial "1" when you dial a phone number domestically (especially from landlines), this is actually the country code for the United States.

You will need to find the country code of the bank you wish to call before you can contact them. Often, especially with banks that cater to an international clientele, they will make this information available on their websites. For the convenience of readers of this book, the country code of each country discussed in Chapter 5 is listed above the map. If the country you are interested in banking with is not listed, simply type the name of the country followed by "country code" into any Internet search engine.

One other concern when calling abroad is cost. International calls can quickly add a healthy amount to any monthly phone bill. One method to combat this problem is to take advantage of new VOIP services. VOIP, which stands for "Voice Over Internet Protocol" is a technology that allows for voice to be transmitted over high speed internet connections. Using a computer with a high speed internet connection as well as a microphone headset, you can quickly, efficiently and inexpensively communicate across the globe at rates that are competitive, if not below, the market rate of traditional phone systems. At the time of this writing, one of the most popular VOIP services for making phone calls through the Internet is a service called Skype (www.skype.com). This service requires the installation of a program as well as the hardware described above. However, it is very easy to use, the call clarity is exceptional, and the pricing is very reasonable.

Interest Restrictions

The banks of many developing nations around the world are happy to take your money on deposit. This money is needed to develop their businesses and supply them with the capital that they need to make loans within their borders. Additionally, as money flows in to the developing banks, it helps to create high paying white collar jobs in the financial services sector. This helps diversify the economies of these countries away from traditional dependencies on tourism and agriculture. This is why, again, so many developing countries, especially small ones, adopt laws and tax policies favorable to international banking. Many of these banks will pay very competitive rates of interest to encourage deposits. At times, these rates can even be higher than the interest rates paid in developed countries. This helps compensate for the higher risk of banking in a developing nation and the frequent lack of a depositor compensation plan.

Often, developing nations will not have personal income taxes and the interest will be paid directly into your accounts. This is not true of foreign banking in developed nations. Most of these countries do have personal income taxes, and this applies to monies received as interest. This can create a problem. As a non-resident, non-citizen of the nation in which you are banking, you will not have a taxpayer identification number. This means that, even if tax were deducted, there is no account at the nation's tax collection service to credit the money. To deal with this problem, developed nations may not allow foreign citizens to bank within their borders without a resident visa (and its associated taxpayer identification number), or if they do, they will not allow you to receive interest payments. This could be a problem if you are making a large deposit. Missing out on even 1% interest on $100,000 on deposit will cost you $1,000 per year! Always make sure you have a complete and thorough understanding of how, when, and if interest will be paid before initiating any banking relationship.

Limits On Services

Many countries around the world have worked very hard to develop international banking sectors in their economies. These countries are often small countries, frequently islands, in the developing world. Candidly, they need your business and deposits for investment in their infrastructures and the jobs that are created. As a result of this need, their banking sectors are cooperative and tailored to work with international customers.

This is not the case of banking industries in developed countries. Many developed countries will not permit you to open an account unless you are a resident of that country. South Korea and The United Kingdom are prime examples.

If a developed country's central bank or bank regulators do permit foreign, non-resident citizens to open an account, there will most likely be limits on the services that you can take advantage of. Be prepared for this. In many cases, there will be a denial of credit lines, as there are no means to verify your credit quality or of the difficulty in pursuing collections activities if you default on a loan.

Residency Requirements

Many countries have limited opening bank accounts to only resident aliens and citizens. To open an account in one of these countries you will need a visa of some kind. This varies widely between countries but can be a temporary visa or a student visa in some cases. For the most current information, contact the consulate of the country you wish to bank in and ask for specifics. To find a consulate simply conduct an internet search.

Examples of countries that require some form of residence visa to open a bank account:

- Great Britain
- Japan
- South Korea
- Italy
- Portugal
- Spain
- The Netherlands
- Mexico
- Israel
- United Arab Emirates
- Brazil

If you have a need of a financial relationship in a country that will not open accounts for foreign, non-residents, the next section discusses a potential work around method to accomplish this.

One Bank, Many Countries

Some banks are so large that they have operations in countries all over the world. Many American, Canadian and European banks fall into this category. If you have a need to establish a banking relationship in a country that requires you to be a resident (you will not qualify with a tourist visa which is generally 30-90 days), these banks may be of great use to you.

Banks of this type are of use in the following way. You can open an account, with one of these banks, in a country that will permit you to do so. This could be your home country, or a foreign country that welcomes foreign bank customers. Once you have established an account in this manner, you have established a banking relationship with that bank, no matter where they conduct their business. At this point, any branch of that bank, that you walk into, will treat you accordingly as a customer of record. The fact that your account is based in a different country will be of little consequence and should not interfere with service. You will be able to access funds on deposit, and receive account assistance and service anywhere in the world this bank operates. Additionally, once you have an established relationship with one of these global banks, it becomes much easier to open accounts with them in other foreign countries, and to move money within their banking system all over the world.

If you have the need to establish a bank account in a country that will not allow foreign, non-residents to do so, you can find a country that is close by in Chapter 5. Next you could carefully examine the lists of banks that operate in both of the jurisdictions, and find one that is on both lists. Then, you would follow the normal procedures of contacting that bank, in the jurisdiction that allows foreign bank customers and explore whether or not opening an account is possible.

Open Just A Savings Account

Checks are a luxury that many Americans take for granted. Many people do not even have a savings account and instead live solely from their checking account. However, around the world checks are considerably less common, and the privilege of check writing is more strictly regulated. You may find that, as a foreign, non-resident; you will not be able to open a checking account. Bluntly, the bank does not want to take a chance that you will use your new check writing ability as a means to commit fraud, or more simply that you will bounce checks all over their country, embarrassingly for them.

There is hope, however, if you can settle on simply opening a savings account. Since you will most likely not even be living in the foreign country in which the account is opened, this should not be a problem. You will not have any need of paying electric or phone bills with checks. You will almost always be issued an ATM with a savings account. This can be used to withdraw cash from ATMs. If you are traveling, you can still use your domestic credit cards to take care of matters such as hotel reservations, and you will find that bankers are often much more willing to open a savings account. With the savings account, you can also still transfer funds from your home country with ease.

The procedure for opening just a savings account is the exact same procedure that you will use to open other account types, however, you will find that many more banks will be willing to work with you. Additionally, in many jurisdictions, including the United States, checking accounts are not paid any interest, however, savings accounts are. This means that, in exchange for not writing checks, your money may actually earn more money in the foreign bank. Of course you will have to pay any applicable taxes on this interest, but this can be a bonus, depending on the size of your deposit.

Currencies and Interest Rate Variance

It is very common to see a difference in the amounts of interest that are paid on term deposits or savings accounts depending on the currency in which the account is denominated. This occurs for several reasons and the rates will fluctuate over time.

The first reason that this happens is due to a variance in demand for the underlying currencies of the deposit. At times, banks may have enough U.S. Dollars on deposit but may need to increase the amount of Euros or Pounds that are in their vaults. To encourage the deposit of these currencies, the bank will offer an increased interest rate for deposits in these currencies.

Additionally, a bank may offer an increased rate of interest to encourage deposits in a weaker local currency. This local currency tends to fluctuate more than the major world currencies and is can be considered "volatile". To make it worth the risk to invest in this currency a higher rate is frequently offered.

The last major reason interest rates vary is due to the inflation associated with that currency. Inflation means the decrease in the purchasing power of money. Each currency in the world has a rate of inflation associated with it. For example, say the United Sates Dollar's inflation rate is 2%. This means next year it will take $1.02 to buy what a dollar bought this year. If the Euro has a 3% inflation rate associated with it, this means that next year you will have to spend €1.03 to buy what €1 bought this year.

Using the numbers from this example, you will need to earn a 2% interest rate on any USD deposits simply to maintain the purchasing power of your money. However, if you are earning 2% on a Euro deposit, you are still losing 1% of your purchasing power each year. You would need to earn at least a 3% rate on any Euro deposits to maintain their value.

The various rates of interest are not just pulled out of thin air, but are the results of the monetary policies of the governments that issue those currencies. Before requesting to open an account, know which currencies a bank will denominate accounts in and which one you wish to bank in. For more information on major world banking currencies, refer back to Chapter 3.

Pack Your Bags

In order to open bank accounts in some foreign countries, you will be required to travel there and conduct you business in person. Examples of countries whose banks may impose this restriction are Canada, Finland and Andorra.

This can be a costly, as well as a time consuming proposition if you must travel half way around the globe to reach the country in question. If money is a problem, you should probably not be considering moving money out of the banks in your home country in the first place. If on the other hand, you are too busy making money and cannot get away, there are many banks in many countries that will be happy to open an account for you through the mail. Many of the Caribbean islands fall into this category. These policies are subject to change, so if you are unsure if this is true, simply ask when you contact the bank you have selected.

If you are dead set on a specific country and have to travel there to open an account, take comfort in the fact, that, while some of the nations that offer international banking services are comparatively poor, they are often rich in natural treasures such as coral reefs and beautiful beaches that are perfect for vacations. If you consider marrying a little pleasure with your banking business and you might have a great time.

Currency Travel Limits

If you are required to travel abroad to conduct your banking business, you should be aware that there are limits on the amounts of currency that you can casually bring with you across a country's border (in or out). The United States limits the amount of currency you can take with you at $10,000 USD. Most other countries follow this example and set their limit closely to this value. As an example, Aruba sets their limit at $11,000 USD which is equivalent to 20,000 Aruban florins.

If you exceed the limit that a country has set, you are required to declare it to both countries' customs bureaus. This should be done well in advance, as you will be required to prove the source of the funds. If you fail to declare the fact that you have exceeded the currency limit, your currency will be seized and may be forfeited. If you plan to move your money to its new home in a foreign country in cash, contact the bank you plan to move the funds to, as well as the customs departments of the two countries that share the border. This will allow you to verify the current laws and procedures and will make sure that you avoid forfeiting your money, and are in compliance with the law.

Opening Accounts Via Mail

In order to open accounts in foreign countries, you will either need to travel to the country in question (as was mentioned), or communicate through the mail. You will not be able to scan and email sensitive documents such as notarized copies of passports. There is too much risk with money laundering and terrorism financing for any bank compliance department to allow this.

Communicating through the national mail service of your country is by far the least expensive option, although some banks may insist on a private carrier service.

You should also be aware that, if the international bank with which you are dealing, chooses to rely on their domestic mail service instead of one of the international carriers previously mentioned, travel times can be as high as two weeks or more. If time is an issue, enquire as to which service they are using and make necessary arrangements if you are unsatisfied with their choice.

Identifying Yourself Across Borders

In the United States, the standard form of identification is a state issued driver's license. This is not the case when traveling or conducting business abroad. The international standard form of identification is the passport. This is true for crossing international boundaries and for identifying yourself to a foreign bank. Before even considering banking abroad, you will need to have a passport in your possession.

If you are not familiar with a passport, this form of ID is a small booklet. Inside, you will find a picture of the bearer along with a physical description and important dates such as a birthday and expiration date of the passport itself, along with personal information. Additionally, many governments, including the United States, are adding microchips to their passports. These chips will contain the same information that is printed in the passport as well as computerized photo of the bearer. Lastly, a passport contains many blank pages that are intended to be used for visa stamps when entering a foreign country.

Unfortunately, in this period of heightened security due to international terrorism, the laws and policies governing the issuance of passports do change from time to time. To find out the most current information regarding the issuance of passports in the United States, visit the State Department's passport homepage at www.travel.state.gov/passport/ . This website will inform you as to the requirements for receiving a passport, identification and proof of citizenship requirements, and fees. Also provided on the website is a searchable database of all the offices in the country where you can apply for a passport. Many post offices offer this service. As of this writing, the fee for a new passport, in the United States, is $100 USD.

In addition to your passport, you will also need to provide your national ID card. In the United States, again, this is your driver's license. However, in many places around the world, a national ID card is required. Some countries even require all of their citizens to obtain a form of national ID as early as age 10.

To open an account, you will need to provide both of these forms of ID in a branch of the foreign bank, or in the form of notarized photocopies (information on notaries is provided in the next section). If you live in a member state of the European Union, and need to open an account in another EU member state, a bank in your home country may be able to accept your ID and verify your identity on behalf of the bank in the foreign country. To find out if this is possible, consult your current EU bank.

Notary Publics

Notary publics will be essential professionals in your efforts to open international bank accounts, especially through the mail. A notary public is a licensed professional, operating under permission from a government, which certifies the authenticity and legitimacy of documents and legal transactions. In essence, they are state certified, professional witnesses. Witnessing the signing of a contract is a typical example of a notary service.

In your efforts to open a foreign bank account, a notary public will be necessary to certify the copies of your identification that you will submit to the foreign bank. Depending on the requirements of the bank or country in which you wish to conduct banking business, you may be required have other documents in the account opening process notarized as well.

One concept that you will need to understand when opening accounts through the mail is that of "signed true originals". A signed true original is a black and white photo copy of your identification that has been notarized. Make sure the copies are black and white; it is illegal to make color copies of ID for security purposes. You can easily make "signed true originals" at most photo copy stores.

Finding a notary public is by no means a difficult process. Many domestic commercial banks, including the ones you currently bank with, will often have a notary on staff. The ability to certify contracts, or mortgages, and other documents is especially useful in the banking business. These notaries will be able to help you as well with your certification needs. There may be a fee, or as a customer, the service may be free. To find out if your bank has a notary on staff and when they are available, simply give them a call. In addition to banks, most business service centers that rent mail boxes, provide copies and accept packages for shipment will also have notaries on staff. They will be happy to help you at a nominal fee.

Letters of Intent

When you wish to open an account with a bank abroad, many of them will ask you to provide them with a letter stating your intention to open an account. This is a "Letter of Intent". This letter will need to be signed by you in the presence of a notary. At that point you will have the notary authenticate the signature and date the document.

These letters are used by many banks in lieu of an application as you would find with a domestic account opening. You should state what type of accounts you with to open, what the accounts will be used for and the amount and method of funding the accounts. Additionally, include what types of identification you are providing. Some banks may also ask you to include your occupation; this is part of the bank's "Know Your Customer" policy. You don't need to make these letters very complicated. Simply state your intention clearly.

Bank Reference Services

Since its introduction, the Social Security Number has become the default means of identification in the United States. With this number and the credit and tax information associated with it, a bank or credit issuer can form a picture of the person applying for credit, by looking at an associated credit report. This stops being true when you leave the United States. When you are conducting business abroad, banks will have no means of checking your credit history and past relationships with banks because their systems are not set up to access the credit reports of foreign customers.

This means, that banks in a foreign country have to form their own picture of you and your credit worthiness and past banking conduct. This can be achieved through a bank reference service.

To obtain a banking reference, the foreign bank will ask you to fill out a simple form that is included with your foreign account opening package. This form gives them your permission to contact banks that you already have a relationship with. It also extends your permission to your current banks to discuss your past relationship with the prospective foreign bank. Without this form banks may not even acknowledge that you are a current customer.

In addition to granting permission to your current bank to discuss your information with the requesting bank, the form also extends permission to debit your current account whatever fee your bank charges for this reference service. You should know this fee in advance before you go and authorize any debits. In most cases, this fee will be under $50, but you should still know in advance.

Most foreign banks will ask you for one or two banking references. If you cannot provide satisfactory references, it is most likely that the foreign bank will choose to not open the requested account.

Bank Introductory Letters

In addition to a bank reference service, or in place of it, you may be required to provide an introductory letter from your local bankers to prospective banks abroad. This service can be provided by most banks; however, the service itself is something that many local banks will be unfamiliar with. You may need to be patient and explain exactly what you want.

There is no standard format to an introductory letter. It will need to be printed on the letterhead of your local bank as well as being signed by a local banker. Do not use a copy, send the original. If you need more than one, or are prudent and want to plan ahead, ask for several copies.

The body of the letter should present you as a customer to the bank abroad. In it, your local bankers should list how long you have been a customer, what types of accounts you have and the fact that you are a customer in good standing. This last part is important. Foreign banks will have no way to check your credit or past banking history, other than by the information you provide to them in letters of this type or other bank references. If you happen to have large deposits at a single bank, include this information as well. Do not include account numbers in the letter. This is unnecessary and could present a security risk. Lastly, make sure that the banker includes their contact information in the letter. If the foreign bank needs further information you want them to be able to get it promptly and with a minimum of trouble.

Declarations Of Source

Foreign banks, as part of their anti-money laundering protocols will often ask you for documentation of the source of the funds that you plan to place on deposit. This is especially true of large deposits. This may require previous bank statements as well as documentation of your sources of income.

Be prepared to provide this documentation if you are asked to do so and be understanding of the bank's need to do this in order to prevent the abuse of the financial system by criminals and terrorists.

Bank Drafts

When opening an account in a foreign country you will need to somehow fund the account. This can be accomplished via a wire transfer, but many foreign banks will ask you to send a check to initiate the account opening process.

It may come as a surprise to you that you can send checks drawn on a domestic bank abroad. However, this is a common and completely acceptable method of funding a foreign account. The easiest way to do this is with a bank draft drawn on your primary bank. A bank draft is simply a printed check guaranteed by the bank. It is really just a bank guaranteed money order. This means that there will be no problems with a handwritten personal check that will only delay the account opening. Checks of this kind can be purchased at any commercial bank for a small fee.

Many large commercial banks even offer foreign currency bank drafts. The currencies that are offered will vary depending on the services of the bank, but all of the major world currencies discussed in Chapter 3 should be available. The fee for a foreign currency bank draft tends to be a little higher than for a bank draft drawn in the domestic currency.

If you do decide to send a check as the means of funding your account, you do need to be prepared for a holding period while the check clears international boundaries. A common amount of time for a procedure like this to take place is between six and ten weeks.

Wire Transfers

A wire transfer is a way to move money between banks instantly. You can move money from an account that you own into an account owned by another individual. This type of wire transfer can be used to pay for something. You can also move money between two accounts that you own. This can be done locally, or just as easily, can be used to move money across the world. You can send funds via wire transfer in either your local currency or a foreign currency.

Any commercial bank will offer wire transfer services. You will need to fill out a form in which you provide both the account number from which the money will be deducted and the account number where the money will be deposited. It will also be helpful to have the physical address of the bank where the funds are being sent.

There are two pieces of information that you need to ask the foreign bank about. These are the SWIFT code and the IBAN number. SWIFT stands for the Society for Worldwide Interbank Financial Telecommunication. This is an electronic system allows for the convenient transfer of funds between participating banks. A SWIFT code is not always needed, but you should ask the receiving bank about it before trying to initiate a wire transfer.

A newer, standard system for international bank transfers is the IBAN, or the International Bank Account Number. This system permits the unique identification of bank accounts across international boundaries. At present, the United States does not participate in the IBAN system, however, many countries around the world do. This number may be required to send money to a foreign bank. Again, ask about it before you attempt to send a wire transfer at a local branch.

Banks will often have cutoff times for business day wire transfers. Any transfer that is scheduled after that point will be sent the next business day. You will also need to pay a fee for the service of a wire transfer. These vary across banks but can be as high as $50 depending on the amount of money that is wired, or the currency in which funds are sent. Wire transfers are a great tool if you are in a hurry to fund an account. However, if time is not a critical factor, you can just as easily send a bank draft.

Online Banking

Online banking is a convenience that most of us have become completely accustomed to. It is a service that is included for free with almost any bank account opening today. Fortunately, the convenience of the Internet is just as accessible when banking across international boundaries. In fact, online banking may be the most convenient form of carrying out transactions with a bank in a foreign country.

Accessing Your Money

Money that is deposited in overseas banks should really be money that is intended for investment in some manner, or money that is used to pay expenses while you are in the country in which it is deposited.. This should not be money that you need to pay rent for your domestic apartment or for your electric bill. If this is the only kind of banking that you carry on, it is probable that offshore banking is not necessarily the right vehicle for you to use. However, at times you may have the need to move some of your overseas funds back into your home country.

There are several ways that you will be able to do this. The first and simplest is to use any ATM or debit cards that were issued to you by the foreign bank. These will only be issued with savings and current accounts. With this card you can withdraw money from an ATM just like with a domestic account. There will of course be an ATM fee from the bank that owns the ATM and most likely there will be a charge from the foreign bank as well. Most banks also charge a fee for any international transactions. You do need to be aware that there will be withdrawal limits in place that prevent you from taking out a large amount. These are in place for your protection to prevent a thief from cleaning out your account before you know what is happening. This fact means that this manner of accessing your funds is really only appropriate for small amounts. Also, before making a series of withdrawals from an ATM that is not in the same country as the bank that you are withdrawing from, you would be wise to call them and advise them of your location. After security verification, they will make a note of your location and the fact that this is authorized activity. If you do not make this phone call, the bank could decide this is suspicious activity, and lock your account for your protection. This is very inconvenient and may require your appearing in person at a bank branch sort the matter out.

A wire transfer is really the most convenient way to retrieve your money from a foreign bank quickly. You will need to contact the foreign bank and make all of the arrangements. You will also need a domestic bank account to act as the recipient of the funds. This will need to be taken care of in advance before requesting the wire transfer.

Conclusion

This chapter presented you with the basic set of tools you will need to open accounts in foreign countries. You now know how to contact foreign banks and whom to speak with. You know what information to request and more importantly, what information the banks will ask for. IBAN numbers and the process of identifying yourself through the mail, as well as many other topics were discussed.

Knowing how to open an account is very a very important part of offshore banking. Looking forward to the next chapter, however, you will learn how to reduce your risk and what you need to be cautious about involving offshore banking.

5

World Banking Almanac

This chapter presents country specific banking information. Some of these countries such as the Cayman Islands, Monaco, and Liechtenstein are well known international banking centers. Others are less well known and are only beginning to develop their banking centers. Others still are not traditional offshore banking centers, but are developed countries that permit their banks to open accounts for foreign citizens. Examples of countries that fall into this last category include Canada as well as Ireland.

Each country profiled will include a basic map indicating where on the globe this particular jurisdiction should happen to fall. Also include will be basic "almanac" style information such as the capital, currency, time code, etc. After this basic information, each country's banking regulators will be listed, as well as links to lists of licensed banks will be provided in many cases. These lists are provided by the bank regulators themselves and are subject to change without notice. Lastly, any relevant or interesting facts such as inclusion in negative OECD listings or the implementation of depositor compensation schemes, or recent bank guarantees will be presented.

Legal Disclaimer

The material presented in this chapter, as well as the books as a whole, is presented for informational purposes only. While all information is thought to be correct, no warranty or guarantee of accuracy is offered. Where information is to be relied upon, it should be independently verified in concert with a licensed attorney.

Andorra

Capital City: Andorra la Vella

Currency: Euro (EUR)

Official Language: Catalan

Time Zone: GMT+1

Calling Code: +376

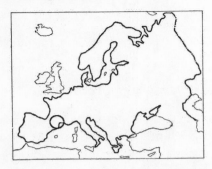

Andorra is a small country located in the Pyrenees Mountains between the borders of France and Spain. This small country of less than 100,000 people has a long, established history going all the way back to its independence in the 13th century.

Andorra is one of Europe's four principalities. Actually, Andorra is a co-principality that is shared between the sitting President of France and the Bishop of Urgell, Spain. At the same time, Andorra is a parliamentary democracy with and elected Prime Minister as its Head of State.

Andorra is a unique place. It is neither Spanish nor French, but has a culture that is uniquely Andorran. Andorra is not part of the European Union, although the official currency is the Euro. Tourism is the mainstay of the Andorran economy as each year millions of tourists flock to the mountain realm to enjoy the area's resorts.

An additional attraction to tourists is the fact that Andorra is a duty free zone. This means many goods can be purchased less expensively than in neighboring European countries. Andorra has no direct taxes on personal assets or income.

Supplemental to its tourist industry, Andorra has a thoroughly developed and modern banking system. The Andorran bank system is similar to the Swiss banking system in that banks are governed by strict bank secrecy laws as well as offering completely integrated financial management services. All banks in Andorra will offer asset management, credit lines, deposit accounts and securities brokerage services.

The Andorran banking system is regulated by the Institut Nacional Andorrà de Finances (www.inaf.ad). This regulatory body oversees the Andorran banking system and assures compliance by regulated bodies with all Andorran laws. The INAF also ensures the stability of the Andorran banking system. According to the INAF, there are currently six licensed banks operating within the Principality of Andorra. Currently the banking system is closed with no new licenses being granted. More information about the Andorran banking system may be found at the website of the Association of Andorran Banks (www.aba.ad).

One fact worth noting for people wishing to deposit money into the Andorran banking system is that all Andorran accounts need to be opened in person. Accounts cannot be opened through the mail. This adds the cost of a trip to Andorra for anyone wishing to avail themselves of the services offered here. However, as was mentioned before, the mainstay of the Andorran economy is tourism. It is entirely possible to finish your banking business by noon and be skiing down the slopes of the Pyrenees shortly afterwards.

Anguilla

Capital City: The Valley

Currency: East Caribbean Dollar (XCD)

Official Language: English

Time Zone: GMT-4

Calling Code: +264

Anguilla is a small island located in the Leeward Islands of the Lesser Antilles in the Caribbean Sea. The island of Anguilla is very small with a total area of less than 40 square miles and about 12,000 inhabitants.

The English were the first to colonize this island in the late 16th century and the island has had a close relationship with the United

Kingdom ever since. This relationship has not always been amicable. There were several rebellions to British rule in the 1960's. In 1980 the island of Anguilla was granted the status of a British Overseas Territory. This is the same political relationship that exists between the Cayman Islands and the United Kingdom. The head of state of the island of Anguilla is Queen Elizabeth II and the islands are ruled through a combination of a British appointed governor and a locally elected government.

Anguilla is also a member of the Organization of Eastern Caribbean States, known as the OECS. The OECS is an economic alliance similar to the European Union. This alliance includes six independent nations in the Eastern Caribbean as well as two British Overseas Territories (Anguilla is one of these). This alliance uses a unified currency known as the East Caribbean Dollar. The OECS also maintains a central bank known as the Eastern Caribbean Central Bank (ECCB) (www.eccb-centralbank.com) on the island of St. Kitts. The role of the ECCB is to ensure the stability of the East Caribbean Dollar by setting monetary policy for the alliance as well as ensuring the stability of the financial systems in the sovereign member nations.

Anguilla's only true natural resources are its beautiful beaches and access to the ocean. This has made the island a popular tourist destination. The fact that the East Caribbean Dollar is pegged to the United States Dollar has made Anguilla a comparatively inexpensive destination as well.

The other driving force behind the Anguillan economy is offshore financial services. Anguilla is a popular location for international incorporation and banking due to the absence of any direct taxation. This means that there is no income, capital gains, or inheritance taxes in Anguilla.

The banking system of Anguilla is monitored by the Financial Services Commission of Anguilla (www.fsc.org.ai). This regulatory body was created in 2003 and began operation in 2004. Today it oversees the banking sector along with mutual funds, insurance companies and other financial institutions.

There are a total of seven licensed banks operating in Anguilla as of this writing. These banks can be found on the website of the Financial Services Authority (www.fsc.org.ai/market.shtml). In reality, there are only five banks. The Trust Companies and Offshore

Banking Act of 2000 required banks to separate their domestic ("onshore") and international ("offshore") accounts. In response to this law the two native Anguillan banks split their operation into four. Each bank now has a domestic operation and a separate international operation. The international banking concerns remain wholly owned subsidiaries of the Anguillan parent banks. In addition to these four operations, there are three other independent banks operating on the island.

Antigua & Barbuda

Capital City: Saint John's

Currency: East Caribbean Dollar (XCD)

Official Language: English

Time Zone: GMT-4

Calling Code: +268

The two islands Antigua and Barbuda (Antigua for short) are another island nation in the Leeward Islands of the Caribbean Sea. Like the neighboring islands of St. Kitts and Nevis, these islands are former colonies of Great Britain and became independent within the last 30 years (1981 to be exact). Antigua is part of the Commonwealth of Nations in the same fashion as Canada, the Cayman Islands and Malta and acknowledges Queen Elizabeth II as the head of state. In addition to being a member of the Commonwealth of Nations (an international cooperative organization made up of former British colonies), Antigua is also a member of the Organization of Eastern Caribbean States and uses the East Caribbean Dollar as its official currency.

Like many of its neighbors, Antigua needed to develop its economy beyond tourism and farming, upon independence. The islands, like others turned to offshore financial services as a convenient means of increasing economic prosperity and government revenues. Legislation permitting international business registration and permitting Antiguan banks to offer financial services abroad were enacted in 1982. The first offshore banks began operation shortly afterwards in 1983. Strict confidentiality laws were also put in place at this time. As with all international confidentiality provisions, there are permitted exceptions when dealing with criminal investigations.

The financial services sector of Antigua is monitored and regulated by the Financial Services Regulatory Commission of Antigua (www.fsrc.gov.ag). A list of banks operating within the jurisdiction is provided on this site as well. Currently, there are 16 licensed deposit companies in Antigua. In addition to offshore banking, Antigua has also made efforts to develop an offshore gaming industry as well. Currently Antiguan law permits the registration and operation of Internet gaming sites from the island.

In 1999, the United States and Great Britain, based on concerns about money laundering activity, enacted a financial advisory against the Antiguan banking system. This was seen as a serious challenge to the health of the offshore financial sector. This advisory was met with new legislation that tightened existing anti-money laundering procedures and implemented new ones. As a result, Antigua was not included in the 2000 FATF list of non-cooperative countries. In 2004 the IMF conducted a review of Antigua's banking system and listed the islands as "compliant" in regards to banking regulation.

Aruba

Capital City: Oranjestad

Currency: Aruban Florin & United States Dollar

Official Language: Papiamento, Dutch, English, Spanish

Time Zone: GMT-4

Calling Code: +297

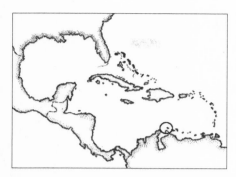

Aruba is a small island in the Caribbean Sea just north of Venezuela. This island was discovered by the Spanish in 1499 and was conquered by the Dutch East Indies Company shortly after. The island has remained a Dutch colony ever since.

Aruba was formerly part of the Dutch Antilles until it voted for autonomy in 1986. Today, it exists, like the Netherlands Antilles, as an independent nation within the Kingdom of the Netherlands. Queen Beatrix II of the Netherlands is the reigning monarch and the government of the Netherlands appoints the islands governor. However, Arubans elect their own legislature and prime minister.

Aruba is not an international banking center in the traditional sense. Due to the fact that many expatriates call Aruba home and many Americans visit the island, it is included in this book. In fact, United States citizens are so common on Aruba that the US Dollar is pegged to the Aruban Florin at a fixed rate and United States Dollars are circulated and accepted everywhere on the island. That being said, the Central Bank of Aruba stipulates that foreign (non-Dutch) citizens can open accounts on the island. However, in order to do so, you must present proof of property ownership on the island.

Supervision of financial institutions is carried out by the Central Bank of Aruba (www.cbaruba.org). This organization also carries out monetary policy as well as the issuance of the Aruban currency and serving as the lender of last resort for the Aruban government.

If you own property in Aruba, and are interested in opening an account, a list of regulated entities can be found at http://www.cbaruba.org/cba/getPage.do?page=SUPERVISION_LIST. As of this writing, there are three licensed commercial banks operating on the island and accounts can be opened for as little as $50 USD.

Austria

Capital City: Vienna

Currency: Euro

Official Language: German

Time Zone: GMT+1

Calling Code: +43

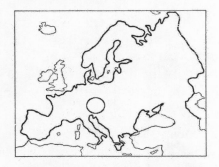

The modern, democratic state of Austria was made independent in 1955, having been reestablished after the defeat of Germany in World War II. However, Austria has a long history of significance on the European stage. For centuries, Austria and its emperors, the Hapsburgs, were considered the bulwark of Europe against invading Turks. After the fall of Napoleon, the map of Europe was redrawn at the Congress of Vienna. Additionally, Austria, most importantly Vienna, has produced many great artists and composers, whose ranks include Mozart, Beethoven and Haydn.

Today, Austria is a modernized, peaceful state located in the heart of Central Europe, boasting a very high per capita GDP. The country did join the European Union in 1995 and uses the Euro as its official currency. However, due to neutrality conditions in the Constitution of 1955, Austria is not a member of NATO. In fact, the neutrality called for in the Austrian constitution is a "permanent neutrality" similar to that practiced by Austria's Western neighbor, Switzerland.

Austria, like many other European countries, is not a traditional offshore banking jurisdiction, but is also a well established and stable economy. Austrian banks are permitted to open accounts for non-residents, however, account opening policies are left to the discretion of the banks themselves.

Banks in Austria are supervised by the Österreichische Finanzmarktaufsicht, or in English the Financial Market Authority or

FMA (www.fma.gv.at). Although the official language of Austria is German, this site has a very good English translation. A list of licensed institutions under supervision by the FMA is available at http://fma.gv.at/cms/site/EN/einzel.html?channel=CH0076.

Before the world banking crisis, deposits in Austrian banks were insured up €100,000 as provided by the Austrian Banking Act. However, amid the world banking turmoil, Austria has made a guarantee of all funds placed on deposit until the end of 2009. As of January 1st 2010, the limit will reduce to the previous €100,000.

The Bahamas

Capital City: Nassau

Currency: Bahamian Dollar (BSD)

Official Language: English

Time Zone: GMT-5

Calling Code: +242

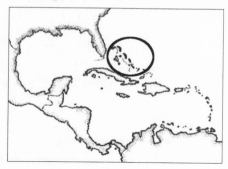

The Bahamas are a numerous chain of islands starting less than 100 miles off the coast of Miami, Florida. These islands lay in shallow Caribbean waters and are an extremely popular destination for tourists and cruise ships. The Bahamas were originally discovered by the Spanish and colonized by the English in the late 17th Century. In the early period of the colony, the many numerous bays, inlets, and small islands became a haven for pirates. The most notable of these seafarers was the notorious Blackbeard. The islands remained a British colony until they were granted full independence by the British Government in 1973. The islands did remain a member of the Commonwealth of Nations and still acknowledge Queen Elizabeth II as the titular head of state. A British Governor, appointed by the Queen still represents Crown interests in the islands. The administrative government is embodied in a parliament and prime minister elected by the people.

Along with tourism, offshore financial services make up the bulk of the Bahamian economy. This has been true since the islands became independent. The close proximity to the United States and even the fact that the financial centers of the United States and the Bahamas share a time zone has helped enormously as well. The Bahamas are so closely associated with the United States that the value of the Bahamian Dollar (BSD) is fixed to the United States Dollar at par. This means that they are exactly equal in value.

Banking regulation in the Bahamas in entrusted to the Central Bank of The Bahamas (www.centralbankbahamas.com). Along with financial regulation, the Central Bank of The Bahamas also issues the currency, sets interest rates in the islands, sets monetary policy, issues bonds, and regulates foreign exchange.

In addition to the duties listed in above, the Central Bank of The Bahamas also administers the island's deposit insurance plan. This plan was enacted in 1999 to protect the stability of the Bahamian banking system. All banks carrying out business in Bahamian Dollars were legally obligated to join the plan. According to the website of the Central Bank, in 2007, there were 14 member banks in the plan. A current list of these banks can be found on the Central Bank website.

Another useful resource for exploring the Bahamian banking system is the Association of International Banks and Trust Companies in the Bahamas (www.aibt-bahamas.com). This is a trade group that represents the interests of international finance companies carrying out business in the Bahamas. This includes representation to the Bahamian government along with codes of conduct for member institutions. A list of member banks is also available on this website.

Barbados

Capital City: Bridgetown

Currency: Barbadian Dollar

Official Language: English

Time Zone: GMT-4

Calling Code: +246

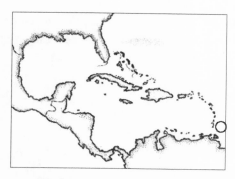

Barbados is a small Caribbean island that lays somewhat to the east of the main Lesser Antilles chain. This coral island was originally discovered by the Spanish in the 16th century, but was not colonized by Europeans until the arrival of the English in the early 17th century. Barbados is unique in the Caribbean islands in that it was never conquered by another European power, but instead remained a British colony exclusively until its independence in 1966.

Today, Barbados exists as a parliamentary democracy that is independent of the United Kingdom. Queen Elizabeth II is the titular head of state. The entire situation is very similar to the relationship shared between the UK and Canada. Barbados is also a member of the British Commonwealth, as is Canada.

For most of its history, the economy of Barbados has been driven by sugar. Sugar was planted by the British shortly after their arrival on the island and it has remained the chief export until the present time. However, in an effort to decouple the economy of Barbados from the unpredictable swings in the price of sugar, the Government of Barbados began to develop an offshore financial services industry. Barbados was aided in this effort by the fact that it shares a time zone with the major United States financial centers. Additionally, the Barbadian Dollar (BBD) has been pegged to the United States Dollar at 1 USD = 2 BBD since 1975.

The offshore industry in Barbados was initiated by the Offshore Banking Act of 1979. This piece of legislation was recently repealed and replaced by the International Financial Services Act 2002-5. Regulation of the financial sector on the island is the responsibility of the Central Bank of Barbados (www.centralbank.org.bb). Banks on the island are licensed in two ways, similarly to the Cayman Islands. Banks are licensed to carry out domestic operations or offshore operations. Currently the central bank lists six domestically licensed banks and fifty seven licensed international operations. Many of these banks are Canadian in origin or are subsidiaries of Canadian banks.

Barbados has also recently instituted a depositor compensation plan. This plan, known as the Barbados Deposit Insurance Corporation or BDCI, was enacted by the Deposit Insurance Act-29 of 2006. The plan, according to the Central Bank of Barbados, is administered by a separate entity and provides up to $25,000 BBD (12,500 USD) in protection to depositors at participating banks. At this time not all banks are participating members of the plan, and this should be thoroughly investigated before any accounts are opened.

Belgium

Capital City: Brussels

Currency: Euro

Official Language: German, Dutch, French

Time Zone: GMT+1

Calling Code: +32

Belgium is a small European country located just to the North of France. Although small by comparison in terms of size, Belgium is an important founding member of the European Union. Additionally, Belgium is home to the North Atlantic Treaty Organization, more commonly referred to as NATO.

Belgium boasts a high per capita GDP, as well as a strong, developed economy. The port of Antwerp is one of the busiest in Europe, as well as the center of the international diamond trade.

Belgium is not a traditional offshore venue, but since it is a popular tourist destination and a significant economy in the European sphere, it is included in this book. More than one hundred banks currently operate within Belgium. Many of the banks are from other European nations around Belgium. The banking system in Belgium is regulated by the Commission Bancaire, Financière et des Assurances (www.cbfa.be). This regulatory body was created in 2004 through the merger of banking and financial market regulators with an existing insurance commission. Detailed information about the current state of the Belgian banking system is available on this site. Included on the site are statistics, lists of banks divided by the licenses and regulation (some banks in Belgium are foreign banks and are governed by the regulatory policies of the foreign governments under EU regulation), as well as current event bulletins concerning the world banking crisis. This site is available in English, as well as French and Dutch, however, since English is not an official language of Belgium; the English language version is more limited.

Like all member nations of the European Union, Belgium has a deposit compensation scheme in place. Prior to October 2008, coverage was limited to €20,000. However, with the advent of the world banking crisis, this amount was raised to €100,000. Details of the plan are available on the website of the CBFA at http://cbfa.be/eng/cob/bd/bd.asp.

Bermuda

Capital City: Hamilton

Currency: Bermudian Dollar (BMD)

Official Language: English

Time Zone: GMT-4

Bermuda: +441

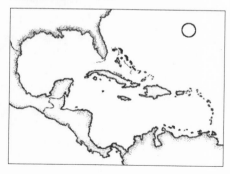

Bermuda is a small island in the Atlantic Ocean located at about the same latitude as the state of North Carolina. Although often referred to singularly Bermuda is actually an island chain made up of many small islands. Bermuda is not technically located in the Caribbean Sea, but is often associated with many of the islands that are.

Bermuda was discovered by Europeans in the early part of the sixteenth century. The islands were first permanently settled by the British and quickly became an important naval base in that country's American colonies.

Today, Bermuda exists as a British Overseas Territory, the same political designation given to Anguilla and the Cayman Islands. Bermuda is ruled by a British governor who is appointed by the island's head of state, Queen Elizabeth II of Great Britain. Bermuda has close ties to both Canada and the United States. The currency of the island, the Bermudian Dollar (BMD) is pegged to the United States Dollar at par. This means that one USD is equal in value to one BMD.

Although the island of Bermuda is small, both geographically and in terms of population (only about 65,000 people call the islands home), Bermuda is a very prosperous country. Some estimates rank Bermuda as having one the highest per capita GDPs in the world. This is largely due to the fact Bermuda has a fully developed and modern financial services sector offering a stock exchange, mutual and hedge funds, offshore incorporation, a competitive international insurance market as well as deposit institutions. Low direct taxation (only import duties, payroll taxes and consumption taxes are collected) and encouraging government policies have also contributed greatly to Bermuda's economic growth.

The banking sector of Bermuda is monitored by the Bermuda Monetary Authority or BMA (www.bma.bm). This regulatory body was established in 1969 with the intention of creating a sound financial system. In addition to monitoring banking activities, the BMA issues the country's money as well as managing currency transactions. Currently there are five organizations licensed to accept deposits on the island. The names and contact information of these entities can be found on the website of the BMA at www.bma.bm/banking/licensed-entities.asp. Each bank will have its own internal policies on foreign accounts. Some banks will only open accounts for foreign citizens who currently live or work in the islands. Others will open accounts for nonresident foreign citizens. Each situation is addressed on a case by case basis by the banks compliance department.

British Virgin Islands

Capital City: Road Town

Currency: United States Dollar

Official Language: English

Time Zone: GMT-4

Calling Code: +284

The British Virgin Islands are the Eastern part of The Virgin Island Chain. The islands are located just to the East of Puerto Rico. The western portion of the chain is an American territory that is separate from the British Virgin Islands.

The British Virgin Islands is a self administered overseas territory of the British Empire and has been since 1967. This administrative designation is the same as the Cayman Islands and Anguilla. The islands currently have about 20,000 residents. Like other British Overseas Territories, Queen Elizabeth II is the head of state and appoints the governor of the territory. Local representation is embodied within the country's parliament and government ministries.

The British Virgin Islands are a very popular jurisdiction for incorporation. According to government publications, a total of more than 400,000 international business corporations are currently formed on the islands. Several factors make the British Virgin Islands attractive for this purpose. Firstly, the island has no capital gains, sales, inheritance, income, or corporate taxation. Secondly, the islands use the United States Dollar as their official currency, even though they are not a part of the United States in any way. Lastly, the time zone on the islands is the same as the East Coast U.S. financial centers.

The financial sector of the British Virgin Islands, along with corporate registration is monitored by the British Virgin Islands Financial Service Commission (BVI FSC) (www.bvifsc.vg). Currently there are a total of nine banks operating from the islands, including two U.S. banks. For a complete list of banks operating in the British Virgin Islands, visit the BVI FSC website at: http://www.bvifsc.vg/RegulatedEntities/Banks/tabid/118/Default.aspx.

Canada

Capital City: Ottawa

Currency: Canadian Dollar (CAD)

Official Language: English and French

Time Zone: GMT-4 to GMT-8

Calling Code: +1

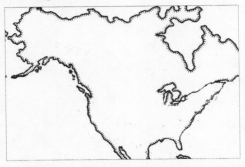

Canada is the northerly neighbor of the United States and occupies the northern third of the North American continent. Canada is a well developed nation and is one of the economic leaders of the Commonwealth of Nations. Like many traditional offshore jurisdictions that are former members of the British Empire, Canada acknowledges Queen Elizabeth II as its head of state. This has been true since the country became independent from Great Britain in 1931.

Canada is not an offshore jurisdiction in the traditional sense. The country has high taxes when compared to the United States and accounts cannot be opened through the mail as a general rule. If these qualities are sought, after consulting the proper tax attorney and financial advisors, you may be better served looking to the offshore operations of many of Canada's international banks in the West Indies. The main reason for the inclusion of Canada in this book is because of its status as the largest trading partner of the United States. Canada and the United States share deep economic ties. This is due largely in part to the sharing of the largest demilitarized border in the world.

As such, many individuals may have cause to establish relationships with banks in Canada. Many Canadian banks will even offer accounts denominated in USD.

Canadian banks are regulated by the Office of the Superintendent of Financial Institutions Canada (www.osfi-bsif.gc.ca). This regulatory body is responsible for setting policies governing deposit taking institutions as well as insurance companies.

As a rule, banks in Canada can open accounts for foreign citizens. However, the rules and restrictions regarding this practice lie with the individual banks themselves. Each institution will have different rules and you will need to address these on a case by case basis. Again, as a rule, you will need to be present in person to open any accounts.

For the most accurate information regarding these policies, consult individual banks. For a list of banks operating in Canada, you can visit the website of the Canadian Bankers Association at www.cba.ca. A list of banks operating in Canada is available on this site as well as many useful publications concerning the Canadian banking system.

Canada also has in place a well developed depositor compensation scheme that is administered by the Canadian Deposit Insurance Corporation (www.cdic.ca). This plan guarantees deposits in participating Canadian banks up to $100,000 CAD.

Cayman Islands

Capital City: Georgetown

Currency: Cayman Islands Dollar (KYD)

Official Language: English

Time Zone: GMT-5

Calling Code: +345

The Cayman Islands are a group of small islands located in the Caribbean Sea just south of Cuba. There are three islands that make up the territory of the Cayman Islands. These islands are known as Grand Cayman, Little Cayman and Cayman Brac. Only Grand Cayman in heavily populated and is the site of the capital city George Town. Georgetown is a popular destination for cruise ships with as many as ten ships coming into port each day during the height of the cruise season.

The Cayman Islands are a British Overseas Territory. Queen Elizabeth II is the Head of State. The Islands are administered by an elected parliament and a governor appointed by the British Government. Unlike the British Virgin Islands, the Cayman Islands issue their own money known as the Cayman Island Dollar (KYD). This monetary unit is fixed to the United States Dollar at a rate of 1 KYD being equal to 1.2 USD.

The focus of the Cayman economy is tourism. The islands boast some of the best scuba diving in the world with visitors coming each year to explore the islands' many reefs. Additionally, cruise ships from the world's most popular lines frequently dock at the islands allowing passengers to experience Grand Cayman's famous Seven Mile Beach. Tourism information on the Cayman Islands is available at the official tourism site, www.caymanislands.ky.

The second large component of the economy of the Cayman Islands is a robust and well develop financial services sector. The Cayman Islands, with a population of around 60,000 people, can boast bank deposits of almost 2 trillion United States Dollars.

The financial system in the Cayman Islands is monitored by the Cayman Islands Monetary Authority (CIMA) (www.cimoney.com.ky). This governmental body is responsible for issuing the currency of the islands, regulating and issuing licenses to the islands financial entities and fighting money laundering.

The financial services sector began to grow in the early 1970's shortly after the island groups break from Jamaica and its designation as a British Overseas Territory. This growth was helped a great deal by the stability offered by the British government and the fact that no direct taxes are levied on the islands. In addition to the lack of local taxes, the Cayman Islands have a long history of discrete private banking as embodied in the Confidential Relationships Preservation Law (CRPL). This law prevents the divulgence of information, by professionals.

However, in an effort to remain a leading world banking center and to prevent the abuse of the system for money laundering and terrorist funding, the Cayman Islands is also very cooperative with foreign law enforcement and tax agencies. The same CRPL allows specific gateways through which information can be released to officials who make formal requests. Additionally, in 2004 the United Kingdom (specifically the Cayman Islands) and the Government of the United States began a program for the sharing of tax information. This makes information regarding criminal tax matters available to United States authorities upon request from the Cayman Islands Monetary Authority.

As of the writing of this book there are 280 licensed banks carrying out operations in the Cayman Islands. Of these banks, 19 are "Category A" banks. These banks are allowed to carry out international and domestic transactions. The remaining 261 banks are "Category B" banks. These banks are restricted to carrying out international transactions only. These entities offer any type of financial service imaginable from deposit accounts in any major world currency to trusts, insurance, and mutual funds. There are even specific companies that will help other companies become listed on the stock exchange. Most of the world's major banks have a presence on the Islands. This includes American, Canadian, British, and Swiss banks. Current lists of licensed banks (updated quarterly) are provided on the CIMA website. You can also search for specific entities and examine their licenses on the same website.

Cook Islands

Capital City: Rarotonga

Currency: New Zealand Dollar

Official Language: English

Time Zone: GMT-10

Calling Code: +682

The Cook Islands are a remote islands chain in the Pacific Ocean to the East of Australia. The Cook Islands became a British colony in 1881 to avoid becoming a French Colony. In 1965, as the British Empire continued to dissolve, the Cook Islands ceased to be a British colony and became a self-governing area in association with the sovereign state of New Zealand.

It needs to be clear that the Cook Islands are not part of New Zealand. Instead, they are essentially a sovereign state that is a protectorate of New Zealand. While the Cook Islands use the New Zealand Dollar as the official currency, the Cook Islands pass their own laws through their own parliament, the government sets its own policies and the islands regulate their own offshore financial center.

Regulatory oversight of banks conducting business in the Cook Islands is vested in the Financial Supervisory Commission of The Cook Islands (www.fsc.gov.ck). Banks, as in many other offshore financial centers, are licensed in two categories. The first of the categories is licensed to conduct business in the islands, specifically of a domestic nature. The other category of banks is licensed to conduct international business dealings such as accepting offshore deposits and trust services. Currently, there are three licensed domestic banks and five internationally licensed banks in the Cook Islands. These banks can be found on the website of the Financial Supervisory Commission website at http://www.fsc.gov.ck/contacts/banks.html. The majority of the banks are major Australian banks conducting offshore banking services.

The Cook Islands were listed as a Non-Cooperative Country or Territory by the FATF in 2000. However, due to the countries implementations of anti-money laundering policies as well as strict customer identification and record keeping practices, the Cook Islands were removed from the NCCT list in 2005. \

Dutch Antilles

Capital City: Willemstad

Currency: Netherlands Antilles Guilder (ANG)

Official Language: Dutch and English

Time Zone: GMT-4

Calling Code: +599

The Dutch or Netherlands Antilles are a group of five islands located in the Caribbean Sea. The five islands of the group are Saint Eustatius, Saba, Saint Maarten, Curacao, and Bonaire. These five islands are spread throughout a wide geographic are in the Caribbean. Saint Eustatius, Saba and Saint Maarten are located in the Lesser Antilles island chain, slightly to the East of Puerto Rico. Bonaire and Curacao, on the other hand are located several hundred miles to the Southwest, just north of Venezuela.

The five islands of the Netherlands Antilles are considered an independent nation that is part of the Kingdom of The Netherlands, like Aruba. This arrangement is similar to the way that Scotland is an integral part of the Kingdom of Great Britain. The neighboring island of Aruba was a member of the Netherlands Antilles until 1986 when its population voted to become a separate independent nation within the Kingdom. The current status of the Netherlands Antilles is not set in stone. Referendums on the relationship each island has with the Netherlands have been held in recent years. Although some of the islands voted for greater autonomy within the kingdom and some voted to become separate countries within the kingdom, no island voted for total independence from the Kingdom of The Netherlands.

The banking system of the Netherlands Antilles is supervised by the Central Bank of Netherlands Antilles (www.centralbank.an). The Central Bank of the Netherlands Antilles also carries out monetary policy for the islands as well as acting as the treasury. The Central Bank also collects tax revenues and issues refunds.

As of this writing, there are a total of ten licensed banks and credit institutions in the Netherlands Antilles. Four of these banks are foreign owned banks operating in the islands or are the subsidiaries of foreign banks. The remaining six banks are local to the Netherlands Antilles. Current lists of these banks as well as contact information for these institutions can also be found on the website of the Central Bank of the Netherlands Antilles.

Banks can be found on the islands that are willing to open accounts for foreign nationals. You will need to submit a notarized copy of your passport as well as a bank reference letter. Accounts can be opened in USD or the local currency, The Netherlands Antilles Guilder (abbreviated ANG and symbolized f). Due to the fact that the United States is the dominant trading partner of the Netherlands Antilles, the Netherlands Antilles Guilder is pegged to the USD at 1 USD = f1.79

Finland

Capital City: Helsinki

Currency: Euro

Official Language: Finnish

Time Zone: GMT+2

Calling Code: +358

Finland is a nation on the Baltic Sea and is one of the Western neighbors of Russia. Finland was actually part of Russia prior to World War I and emerged after the collapse of the Russian Monarchy as an independent nation. Today, Finland is a member of the European Union and has been one of that alliance's most productive economies. GDP in Finland is comparable on a per capita basis to other, large members of the EU. A large portion of Finland's GDP is generated through the export of goods and service throughout the Baltic region and the rest of the world.

Finland is not a traditional international financial center, however, banks in Finland are permitted to open account for non-resident foreigners. However, in most cases, banks will insist on opening any accounts in person.

The banking system in Finland is monitored and regulated by the Finnish Financial Supervisory Authority, or FIN-FSA (www. http://www.finanssivalvonta.fi/eng/). This agency was newly created in 2009 and replaced the previous Finnish Financial Supervision Authority (please note a different form of the word "supervise"). The old Finnish Financial Supervision Authority Website is no longer being updated; however, the list of banks presented on the website at http://www.rahoitustarkastus.fi/Eng/About_us/Supervised_entities_an d_notifications/commercial_banks.htm is being updated. Most likely as the Financial Supervisory Authority matures, this list will migrate to the new website.

The Finnish Deposit Guarantee Fund provides the depositor compensation plan for Finland. In 2008, the coverage limit was raised from €25,000 to €50,000 per institution. This level of coverage will remain in effect at least until the end of 2009. For more information on the Finnish deposit guarantee program, visit http://www.fin-fsa.fi/Eng/Customer_protection/Funds/etusivu.htm.

France

Capital City: Paris

Currency: Euro

Official Language: French

Time Zone: GMT+1

Calling Code: +33

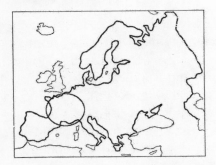

France is not a traditional "offshore jurisdiction"; however, France has an extremely robust economy, a thoroughly developed financial system. The country is one of the stout pillars upon which the European Union rests. France is also one of the developed European countries, like Finland, that will permit its banks to open accounts to non-resident foreign citizens.

The financial system of France is administered and regulated by the French central bank, the Banque de France (www.banque-france.fr), in partnership with the European Central Bank in Frankfurt, Germany. Specifically, within the Banque de France, the actual regulatory body for banks is the Comité des établissements de credit et des entreprises d'investissement or CECEI. Information regarding the CECEI, its activities and responsibilities, and authorized banks is available at http://www.banque-france.fr/cecei/gb/index.htm. This webpage is presented in French by default; however, it is also available in an English version.

There are many banks operating in France and their policies will all be different regarding foreign citizen account opening. For specific information, you will need to contact a branch and go from there. Make sure that you have a thorough understanding of any account fee structures before opening the account. Additionally, as a foreign national, you may not qualify for interest, as again, this would need to be taxed by the French government.

As France is a well developed country with an advanced banking system, there is a deposit insurance plan in place. This plan was established by the law in 1999 and is applicable to all banks that are headquartered in France or in the Principality of Monaco. To review the law itself, visit the Banque de France website at http://www.banque-france.fr/gb/supervi/telechar/regle_bafi/Regulation_99_05.pdf. Currently, the maximum insurable amount is set to €70,000. For more information concerning the plan, as well as current members, visit the Fonds de Garantie des Depôts at www.garantiedesdepots.fr.

Germany

Capital City: Berlin

Currency: Euro

Official Language: German

Time Zone: GMT+1

Calling Code: +49

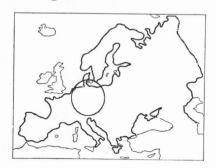

The modern Federal Republic of Germany was created in 1990 after the reunion of West Germany to East Germany amid the breakup of the Soviet Union. The fall of the infamous Berlin Wall at the hands of East Germans was watched around the world and captured the imagination of a generation of Germans. Today, Germany, along with France, is the driving force of the economy of the European Union. In fact, the European Central Bank, which is responsible for monetary policy throughout the Eurozone is located in Frankfurt, Germany.

Germany, like most of the European Union countries is not a traditional offshore jurisdiction, but is a popular destination with world travelers and has significant trading relationships with the United States and many other countries around the globe. Due to these facts which create an interest in establishing bank relationships, Germany is included in this work. Non-residents are permitted to open accounts in Germany, however, some banks will choose not to do so based on their internal policies while others will.

The German banking sector is regulated by the Bundesanstalt für Finanzdienstleistungsaufsicht known in Germany as the BAFin. IN English, this agency is referred to as the German Federal Financial Supervisory Agency (www.bafin.de). The BAFin is an excellent source of information for the more than 2,000 banks currently operating within the borders of Germany. This site includes searchable databases and part of the site is in English, however, much of the information is available in German only, so knowledge of that language would be very helpful. A complete list of all banks operating in Germany is available in spreadsheet form is available at http://www.bafin.de/cln_109/nn_720794/SharedDocs/Downloads/DE/Verbraucher/Recherche/li__080115__ki.html.

Germany, as a founding member of the European Union and one of its financial leaders has in place a strong bank guarantee system. Prior to October of 2008, the upper limit of the German compensation plan was set at 90% of deposits up to €20,000. However, amid the world banking crisis, the EU raised the lower limit of deposit insurance coverage to €50,000. The German government at this time has guaranteed all private savings deposits in order to allay any panic over deposited funds. As of this writing, the situation has not clarified and is likely to continue to evolve. For the most current information on deposit insurance coverage in Germany visit the BAFin website or The Association of German Banks at www.bankenverband.de/einlagensicherung.

Gibraltar

Capital City: Gibraltar

Currency: Gibraltar Pound (GIB)

Official Language: English

Time Zone: GMT+1

Calling Code: +350

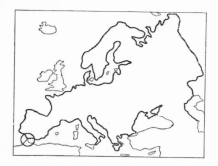

Gibraltar is a small strip of land (on about 2.5 square miles) at the Southern tip of the Iberian Peninsula where the Atlantic Ocean and Mediterranean meet.

Gibraltar was annexed by the British at the beginning of the 18th Century from Spain. Ever since the annexation, the possession of Gibraltar has been a point of contention between the two countries. The British, however, have maintained control of Gibraltar both for its strategic location at the mouth of the Mediterranean and due to expressed will of the inhabitants. Today, Gibraltar exists as a British Overseas Territory.

Banking and financial services make up almost one third of Gibraltar's economy. There are currently almost fifty licensed institutions that can accept deposits. The stability of the financial system is protected and regulated by the Financial Services Commission of Gibraltar (www.fsc.gi). The FSC website contains a wealth of information about banking in Gibraltar as well as anti money-laundering laws in effect. Gibraltar has worked very hard to develop a robust, well respected   international banking center. They have been very successful in attracting banking operations from all over the world. A list of banking operation in Gibraltar is available on the FSC website at http://www.fsc.gi/fsclists/bnklist.asp.

Gibraltar also has in place a Depositor Compensation Scheme and has since 1998. This plan is referred to as the Gibraltar Deposit Guarantee Scheme and is admixture by the Gibraltar Depositor Guarantee Board (www.gdgb.gi). This plan offers protection of up to 90% of the deposits, per individual, to a maximum of £18,000 or €20,000. Not all banks participate in the plan and not all deposits are covered. As of this writing, a total of 12 banks participate in the plan. For more information on the Gibraltar Deposit Guarantee Scheme, visit the Board website listed above or consult the law itself at http://www.gibraltarlaws.gov.gi/articles/1998-08o.pdf.

Grenada

Capital City: Saint George's

Currency: East Caribbean Dollar (XCD)

Official Language: English

Time Zone: GMT-4

Calling Code: +473

Grenada is a small independent island nation at the Southern end of the Antilles chain in the Caribbean Sea. The Island of Grenada is located just to the North of Trinidad and the South of Saint Vincent & The Grenadines Islands.

Grenada became a British colony in the middle of the 17th Century and remained so until the island's independence in 1974. With a total population of less than 100,000 people, Grenada remains one of the smallest nations in the Western Hemisphere.

Grenada entered onto the world stage in 1983, when with Cuban assistance, a local Marxist group seized control of the island. Six days later, a U.S. led, multinational force invaded the island and restored free elections. Free elections have continued to this day.

The economy of Grenada has struggled since this event and a series of subsequent hurricane disasters. Nutmeg agriculture (the main export of Grenada) as well as tourism have suffered as a result and the local government has relied on public debt to rebuild. As of 2009, according to the CIA World Factbook, the public debt of Grenada exceeds annual GDP.

As one of the means to aid in the recovery of Grenada, as well as to draw in needed international capital, Grenada has developed an offshore financial industry. The industry is small, with only a total of five licensed banks. Of the five licensed banks, only a one of them is a local Grenadian bank. The other four banks are licensed foreign banks that are operating on the island or are foreign owned subsidiaries.

Due to the fact that Grenada is a member nation of the Organization of Eastern Caribbean States, banks in Grenada are regulated by the Eastern Caribbean Central Bank (www.eccb-centralbank.org) located in Saint Kitts. There are local offices of the ECCB on Grenada as well as a local financial regulatory office, the Grenada International Financial Services Authority. Both offices are located in Saint George's. Current contact information can be found on the ECCB website as well as contact information for the licensed banks on the island.

Guernsey

Capital City: Saint Peter Port

Currency: Great British Pound & Locally issued Pounds

Official Language: English & French

Time Zone: GMT

Calling Code: +44-1481

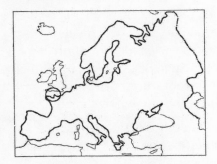

The Island of Guernsey together with the Island of Jersey, form what are collectively known as the Channel Islands. Although, these two islands are often referred to as a single entity, it is important that the reader understand that these islands are politically separate jurisdictions, although they have a great deal in common.

Guernsey is a protectorate of the United Kingdom that sits in the English Channel, just west of the Cotentin Peninsula of France. Guernsey, along with Jersey form the Duchy of Normandy. The Duchy of Normandy was originally a possession of William the Conqueror, who became King of England in 1066. In 1204, after a long period of dispute with the French King, the French conquered the continental portion of the Duchy and claimed it as a possession of the French Crown. The Kings of England were only left with the two islands off the coast. The islands were never incorporated into the United Kingdom and remain solely a Crown Dependency. Additionally, Guernsey is not a member of the European Union. Queen Elizabeth II also maintains the title of Duke of Normandy.

Like many other small countries, the Channel Islands have found prosperity through welcoming international banking operations. Today, there are more than forty international banks operating from the island. Most of these banks are European; however, well known banks from the United States and Canada, among others also conduct business from Guernsey. As of September 2008, according to Guernsey government publications, there was a total of £136.3 billion on deposit in Guernsey banks, with more than 40% of that total being fiduciary deposits from banks in other countries.

Banking operations in Guernsey are monitored and regulated by the Financial Services Commission of Guernsey (www.gfsc.gg). The FSC of Guernsey was created in 1994. As with most Financial Services Commissions around the world, the FSC of Guernsey is in charge of protecting the financial system. A great deal of current information is available on the website of the FSC including alerts and updates to the baking system. You can also find a complete list of all the banks operating on the island at http://www.gfsc.gg/content.asp? pageID=79&menuOpen=1&submenuOpen=1.2. Banks operating in Guernsey are permitted by the FSC to open accounts for foreign nationals, however, each bank is allowed to set its own policies. For current policies from a specific bank, use the contact information provided by the FSC website.

One recent development concerning banking in Guernsey was the introduction of a Depositor Compensation Scheme. This new law came into effect on November 26th 2008, in response to the global banking crisis and the failure of the Icelandic banking system. This law, Billet D'Etat XIX 2008, provides for £50,000 in coverage *per depositor per bank*. This coverage is only available to retail depositors meaning corporate depositors are not offered this protection, however, the retail depositors can be both local and non-local. This plan is funded through fees charged to licensed banks and through insurance. This move was specifically aimed at preserving the reputation of Guernsey as a leader in the international banking industry.

Hong Kong

Capital City: Hong Kong

Currency: Hong Kong Dollar (HKD)

Official Language: Chinese & English

Time Zone: GMT+8

Calling Code: +852

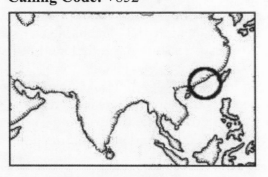

Hong Kong is a former British colony that was reincorporated into The People's Republic of China (PRC) in 1997 as a "Special Administrative District". Before the re-absorption of Honk Kong, the British administered colony had earned a well deserved reputation as one of the leading financial centers of East Asia. This tradition has continued since 1997, with more than 200 banks from all over the world carrying out operations in Hong Kong.

Hong Kong lies on a peninsula on the Eastern side of the Pearl River Delta. Historically this area has been a used as an entry point for foreign goods into China. This was the main reason for the British occupation of the area following The First Opium War in the 19th Century. However, since China opened to the West in the 1970's the Pearl River Delta has become one of China's most productive manufacturing and export centers. This fact, combined with the world renowned financial services sector of Honk Kong, has permitted a large inflow of foreign capital into the region which currently serves as one of the driving engines of the Chinese economy.

Banking in Hong Kong is regulated by the Hong Kong Monetary Authority (www.info.gov.hk/hkma/index.htm). This agency not only regulates Hong Kong's banks, it is also responsible for monetary stability in the district, and the issuance of the Hong Kong Dollar. The Hong Kong Monetary Authority issues three distinct types of licenses to deposit taking institutions. These are licensed banks, restricted license banks, and deposit taking companies. Only institutions that have been deemed a licensed bank are permitted to establish current and savings accounts. Lists of licensed institutions are available on the Hong Kong Monetary Authority website at www.info.gov.hk/hkma/eng/bank/index.htm. These lists are presented in the form of a spreadsheet document.

It should also be noted that the Hong Kong Dollar is one of the most commonly traded currencies in the world on world currency exchanges. The Hong Kong Dollar, abbreviated HK$ or HKD, was pegged to the United States Dollar in 1983 and remains so to this day at a rate of 1 USD to 7.75 HKD.

Hong Kong has also established a depositor compensation plan. This plan is administered by the Hong Kong Deposit Protection Board (www.dps.org.hk/en/home.html) and provides for $100,000 HKD in coverage for all qualified account regardless of the currency held in the account. Like many other governments in Asia and the world as a whole, this amount has been increased to the full deposit amount until the end of 2010. For more information and the most current state of the plan, visit the board website.

Ireland

Capital City: Dublin

Currency: Euro (EUR)

Official Language: Irish and English

Time Zone: GMT

Ireland: +353

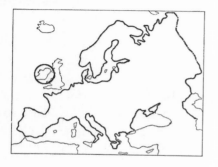

The Irish Republic gained independence from Great Britain in 1921 through partition of the island. The areas in the Northeast of the island, whose population were majority Protestant, voted to remain part of the United Kingdom.

The Irish republic was one of the founding members of the European Union in 1993. Ireland adopted the Euro in 2002 when the currency began circulation. Beginning in the late 1990's and aided by a young, well educated population and a government that has focused on economic development, the Irish Republic has grown its economy to one of the highest per capita GDPs in the European Union and the world as a whole.

The Irish banking system has grown in prominence around the world with the country's economy. Today there are many, many banks from all over Europe and the rest of the world carrying out operations on the Irish Isle. Financial policies in Ireland are governed by the Central Bank of Ireland in conjunction with the European Central Bank (www.centralbank.ie). This website can provide detailed statistics on the Irish banking system as a whole, as well as current trends in savings and debt. Licensed banks in the country are regulated and monitored by the Irish Financial Regulator (www.financialregulator.ie). The mandate of this government organization is to protect consumers through education about financial products as well as ensuring the soundness of licensed institutions. A current list of the banks licensed by the Irish Financial Regulator is also available on this site.

Prior to September 2008 deposits in Irish banks were guaranteed up to €20,000. However, in late September 2008 in response to the evolving global financial crisis, the Irish government increased this coverage to €100,000. This may change further. For the most current information on the Irish Deposit Guarantee Scheme, visit the Irish Financial regulator website.

Opening a bank account in Ireland may be somewhat more complicated than other international banking transactions. Ireland is not an "offshore" banking center per se, but simply a foreign country. Irish banks can open accounts for non-residents, but the decision to do so and the requirements of account opening, as is often the case, are based on each bank's own policies. All of the banks will require a depositor to open the account in person.

Isle of Man

Capital City: Douglas

Currency: Pound Sterling (GBP)

Official Language: English and Manx

Time Zone: GMT

Calling Code: +44-01624

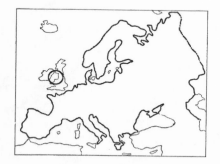

The Isle of Man is a small island located in the middle of the Irish Sea which separates the islands of Great Britain and Ireland. The Isle of Man is a dependency of the British Crown. Although, not formally part of the United Kingdom, the Isle of Man is closely associated with Great Britain. Queen Elizabeth II is the formal head of state with the tile of "Lord of Man" (in addition to "Duke of Normandy") and the government of Great Britain handles the island's foreign affairs. Additionally, the island is permitted to mint its own version of Great British Pounds known as the Manx Pound. The Manx Pound is interchangeable with other British Pounds at a one to one parity. The Isle of Man is not part of the European Union, although it is nominally associated with the EU through its relationship with Great Britain.

Financial services make up a large part of the economy of the Isle of Man. Banks and banking customers are drawn to the island due to the favorable tax policies of the island's government. There is no capital gains tax, wealth tax or inheritance tax on the island. Income taxes rates are capped and the maximum amount of taxable income for individuals is set at £100000.

The financial services sector of the Isle of Man is regulated by the Financial Supervision Commission of The Isle of Man (www.fsc.gov.im). Currently there are 41 registered banks operating on the Isle of Man. Most of the banks are British, Scottish or Irish in origin and many are major international banks. The names of these banks, as well as all other financial entities regulated by the FSC can be found on the website of the Government of The Isle of Man at http://www.gov.im/fsc/licence/licenceholders.xml.

The policies regarding opening bank accounts for foreign citizens vary widely on the Isle of Man. Each bank will have its own policies over who can take advantage of their services. However, you can find banks that are willing to open account through the mail and with wire transfers. Accounts can be opened for as little as $2,000 USD, although interest may not accrue until deposits are at levels approaching $50,000 USD.

The Isle of Man does have a deposit compensation plan in place. This plan is administered by the Financial Supervision Commission of the Isle of Man. All licensed banks operating within the Isle of Man are participants in the plan. The plan currently will provide a maximum payout in the event of default of £50,000 per depositor, irrespective of the nationality of the depositor. For the most current information, consult the FSC website listed previously.

Jersey

Capital City: Saint Helier

Currency: Great British Pound & Locally issued Pounds

Official Language: English & French

Time Zone: GMT

Calling Code: +44-1534

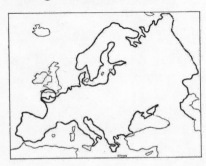

The Island of Jersey is the second part of the Channel Islands and together with its sister island, Guernsey, makes up the Duchy of Normandy. Jersey is the larger of the two islands with about 90,000

inhabitants. Like its sister island, Jersey has been a British protectorate and Crown Dependency since the fall of the continental portion of the Duchy to the French in 1204. Jersey is not part of the European Union and prints its own version of British Pounds.

Also, similarly to the Island of Guernsey, Jersey has built a robust economy through welcoming international banking concerns. There are currently 47 international banks operating from the island. The banks are primarily European in origin; however, banks from the United States, Canada, India and the Middle East all have operations here. The banks that operate from Jersey are some of the largest banks in the world. Only banks that can be counted among the world's largest 500 banks are permitted to operate from the island.

The financial industry on the Island of Jersey is regulated and monitored by the Jersey Financial Services Commission (www.jerseyfsc.org). The FSC is responsible for protecting the reputation and image of the island's financial industry as well as preventing financial crimes on the island. The FSC also provides a list of all licensed banks operating from the island on their website at http://www.jerseyfsc.org/banking_business/regulated_entities/index.asp.

Banks operating in Jersey are permitted to open accounts for foreign nationals, however, there is a rigorous screening process that will require you to declare the source of the funds being placed on deposit, as well as properly identify yourself and make clear your current tax status. Based on this information the bank will decide whether or not to accept you as a client.

As of this writing, there is no depositor compensation scheme in place in Jersey; however, a plan is under active consideration by the islands legislature and banking regulators.

Liechtenstein

Capital City: Vaduz

Currency: Swiss Franc (CHF)

Official Language: German

Time Zone: GMT+1

Calling Code: +423

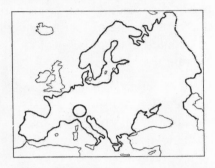

Liechtenstein is a small sovereign country that is landlocked between Switzerland and Austria. Although small, with around 35,000 citizens during the last census, Liechtenstein boasts a very high GDP with a per capita income of more that $50,000 USD.

Liechtenstein is a hereditary principality with the Liechtenstein family currently occupying the throne. In 1924, following World War I, Liechtenstein entered into a customs union with Switzerland. This arrangement has lead to a close political relationship with Switzerland including the use of the Swiss Franc as the country's official currency.

Liechtenstein, like its neighbor Switzerland, has a long tradition of banking. Today, the principality can proudly compare its banking industry with those of other developed and modern nations. According to the Portal of the Principality of Liechtenstein (www.liechtenstein.li) financial services account form more than 30% of GDP in Liechtenstein and employs 14% of the working population. As of this writing, more than 170 billion Euros in assets were under management in the Liechtenstein banking system.

The banking system of Liechtenstein is regulated by the Financial Market Authority of Liechtenstein (www.fma-li.li). This regulatory body is independent of the banking community and reports only to the parliament of Liechtenstein. The Financial Market Authority of

Liechtenstein exists to protect the stability of the financial system as well as its clients and to ensure the reputation of the banking system in the global community.

Banks operating in Liechtenstein will offer any of the services of a major banking system from deposit accounts, to credit cards and lines of credit. Some of these banks will offer deposit boxes as well as precious metal deposit services. You do need to understand that the banks in Liechtenstein are primarily investment banks and will tend to focus on their core business of asset management.

Licensed banks operating in Liechtenstein can be found on the website of the Liechtenstein Banker's Association at www.bankenverband.li. This site is very user friendly and is available in English. All of the member banks (there are 15 as of this writing) are listed with full contact information. While German is the official language all of the websites are accessible in English as well.

Liechtenstein has established a deposit guarantee scheme through the Liechtenstein Banker's Association. This plan is known as the "Deposit Guarantee and Investor Protection Foundation of the Liechtenstein Bankers Association". The plan currently provides up to €20,000 in protection. For the most current information about the plan, visit the website of the Lichtenstein Banker's Association.

Luxembourg

Capital City: Luxembourg

Currency: Euro (EUR)

Official Language: German & French

Time Zone: GMT+1

Calling Code: +352

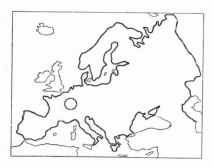

The modern Grand Duchy of Luxembourg was created by The Congress of Vienna after Napoleon's defeat at Waterloo. This was a compromise that ended the territorial claims of both France and Prussia (modern Germany). Today, Luxembourg, or more properly the Grand Duchy of Luxembourg exists as a landlocked, stable, westernized constitutional monarchy. The Grand Duchy is both a member of NATO as well as a founding member of the European Union. The Euro was adopted in 1999.

Almost half a million people reside within the country, which possesses a thriving economy that benefits from trade with Luxembourg's neighbors France, Belgium and Germany. Luxembourg is also home to a thriving financial sector, which alone accounts for more than a quarter of the country's GDP. Many of the more than one hundred banks operating in Luxembourg are foreign owned and foreign, non-resident citizens are permitted to open accounts. As always, individual banks are permitted to set policies according to their own standards.

Banking in Luxembourg is controlled by the Commission de Surveillance du Secteur Financier or CSSF (www.cssf.lu). This organization exists to protect the soundness and reputation of the Luxembourg financial sector. A list of banks operating in Luxembourg is available on the website under the "Supervised Entities" menu option. Monetary policy within the Grand Duchy is carried out by the Central Bank of Luxembourg (www.bcl.lu), in partnership with the European Central Bank in Frankfurt.

As an EU member country, Luxembourg has established a deposit guarantee scheme, which is administered by the Association pour la Garantie des Dépots Luxembourg or AGDL (www.agdl.lu). All banks operating in Luxembourg are legally bound to participate in this program, which provides €100,000 in coverage per depositor, regardless of the nationality of the depositor or the currency in which the deposit is held.

Macao

Capital City: Macao

Currency: Macanese Pataca

Official Language: Chinese & Portuguese

Time Zone: GMT+8

Calling Code: +853

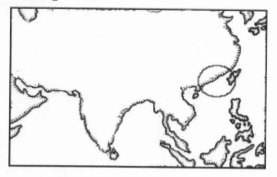

To the West of Hong Kong, across the mouth of the Pearl River Delta, lies another former European colony that has become a special administrative district of the People's Republic of China. This former Portuguese colony is known as Macao, also often spelled Macau.

Macao was the first European colony in China, established in 1557. Portuguese colonists continued to arrive in Macao, which was rented by the Portuguese from the Emperor of China. Following the First Opium War, Macao, like Hong Kong to the British, was signed over to the Portuguese as a concession. In 1999, after 442 years, Macao was returned to the Chinese government by Portugal.

During its years of European colonization, Macao grew prosperous through international finance and a stable government. Almost thirty licensed banks currently operate in Macao, under the supervision of the Monetary Authority of Macao or AMCM (www.amcm.gov.mo). Additionally as of June 2008, according to the AMCM, banks in Macao held in assets totaling more than USD 39 Billion. Along with supervising financial institutions in Macao, the AMCM also issues and sets policy the territory's currency Macanese Pataca (MOP). Although Macao does issue its own local currency, most financial transactions take place in one of the dominant world currencies. A comprehensive list of banks operating in Macao is available at www.amcm.gov.mo/banking_sector/bank.htm.

At the current time, there is no deposit insurance scheme in place in Macao, although the government of Macao has guaranteed all funds deposited in Macao banks (exclusive of offshore banks) until the end of 2010. At that point, it is anticipated that Macao will introduce a comprehensive deposit guarantee scheme.

Malta

Capital City: Valletta

Currency: Euro (EUR)

Official Language: Maltese and English

Time Zone: GMT+1

Calling Code: +356

Malta is a pair of inhabited islands located in the Mediterranean Sea, about fifty miles south of the Island of Sicily. The islands have a long history from the prehistoric to the modern day. The two most famous episodes both deal with the islands refusals to submit to conquest. The Knights of St. John were given the islands as a fief in 1530 by the Spanish Crown. In recognition, the knights gave the Spanish King, each year, a falcon in payment. This is the origin of the famous "Maltese Falcon". In 1565, the knights successfully defended the islands from a massive Turkish invasion. Malta became a British Territory after the conclusion of the Napoleonic Wars and became a major British Naval base in the Central Mediterranean. In 1940, Malta defended itself from a German blockade and bombing campaign more intense than the London Blitz. In recognition of this feat, the entire territory was awarded the George Cross after the siege. This cross, adorns the red and white fields of the national Maltese flag today.

Today Malta is a modern nation with a lovely blending of Mediterranean culture and British charm. The Maltese observe the custom of the siesta and offices and attractions are closed midday for this purpose. The Maltese speak the Maltese language, which is a 10th century dialect of Arabic. However, owing to the country's past association with Great Britain, English is also an official language of the islands. You will have no problems whatsoever conducting affairs in English.

Malta was admitted to the European Union in 2004 and the official currency of the country is now the Euro. Monetary policy in Malta is carried out by the Central Bank of Malta (www.centralbankmalta.org), in concert with the European Central Bank (www.ecb.int). The Central Bank of Malta was established shortly after Maltese independence in 1968 and also acts as the lender of last resort for the Maltese banking system.

The Maltese banking system itself is overseen by the Malta Financial Services Authority (MFSA) (www.mfsa.com.mt). This regulatory body is fairly new and was only established in 2002. This body oversees all financial institutions from credit issuers to banks and investment retailers and advisors. As of this writing, there are 21 listed credit institutions in Malta. A list of these banks can be found on the MFSA website by searching for credit institution license holders. Most of the banks are European in origin but Malta can boast of several internationally recognized homegrown banks. As of 2004, Malta terminated all offshore banking licenses. All banks currently conducting operations in Malta have a physical presence in the islands and are subject to the direct regulation of the MFSA.

Malta, like most developed banking centers has strict conduct rules regarding information sharing. These responsibilities are spelled out in the Maltese Professional Secrecy Act. Information is held in confidence except when in conjunction with a criminal investigation or regarding tax matters. Additionally, Malta has strong identification and record keeping policies in place to reduce the threat to the financial system from money laundering. A Financial Intelligence Unit is in place as well to investigate suspicious transactions.

Malta also instituted the Maltese Depositor Compensation Scheme in 2003 as part of EU admission. This fund is similar in nature to the FDIC program, in that banks pay into a central fund that is used to compensate depositors in the event of a bank failure. For the most current information concerning the Maltese Depositor Compensation Scheme, visit www.compensationschemes.org.mt.

Monaco

Capital City: Monaco

Currency: Euro

Official Language: French

Time Zone: GMT+1

Calling Code: +377

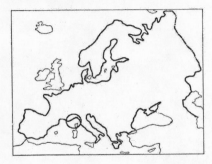

Monaco is a small independent principality located on the southern coast of Europe bordering the Mediterranean. The Principality of Monaco has been ruled by the Grimaldi Dynasty since the 13th Century, when the founder of the dynasty seized the local fortress by masquerading himself and his forces as monks. Since the 13th Century the Principality has gained a reputation of prosperity. Many wealthy individuals throughout the world call Monaco home thanks in large part to its policy of low taxation. Additionally, tourist from all over the world visit Monaco each year to experience the charms of this small territory, as well as its famous Monte Carlo Casino, located in the heart of the French Riviera.

Monaco and its banking system cater to the extremely wealthy and have since the tax laws of the country became so favorable in the 19th Century. Many celebrities and business elite call Monaco home and create a culture with an extremely high standard of living.

Since its founding, the Grimaldi family and the Principality of Monaco have maintained a close association with France. France provides for the military defense of Monaco as well as regulating financial institutions in Monaco through the Bank of France. All of the banks in Monaco must be licensed by the Bank of France. Indeed, many of the banks that have operations in Monaco are of French origin. Additionally, deposit compensation plans and guarantees in place in France also apply in Monaco.

For more information on banks in Monaco, consult the "France" section of this chapter.

Montserrat

Capital City: Plymouth and Brades

Currency: East Caribbean Dollar (XCD)

Official Language: English

Time Zone: GMT-4

Calling Code: +664

Montserrat is a small volcanic island in the Lesser Antilles chain of the Caribbean Sea. Originally claimed by Christopher Columbus and named after a monastery in Spain, this island was settled by Irish immigrants in the early 17th Century. The island became a British colony and has remained part of the United Kingdom. The Irish influence on Montserrat is palpable to this day. Banks are closed on Saint Patrick's Day and the logo of the Financial Services Commission includes a traditional Irish harp.

In the last decades of the 20th Century, Montserrat suffered a pair of disasters that have left the island economically battered. The first of these disasters was the devastating landfall of Hurricane Hugo in 1989.

In 1995, the previously dormant volcano on the island sprang to life. These changes lead to a violent eruption that buried much of the island, including the capital city, in ash and lava. At this point the island's government relocated to Brades. This is the de facto capital of the island as of this writing. This added to the woes of the island that was still rebuilding from Hugo. Due to these events and economic conditions on the island, Montserrat is the only British Overseas Territory whose citizens enjoy full United Kingdom Citizenship with residency rights. This change was implemented in 2002.

Montserrat is a member state of the Organization of Eastern Caribbean States, just as Anguilla is, even though it is not an independent nation. As such, the banking system is regulated by the East Caribbean Central Bank (www.eccb-centralbank.org) like other nations in the group. Two licensed banks are currently listed on the ECCB website. One is a bank local to Montserrat and the other is a Canadian Bank. Local regulation is carried out the Financial Services Commission of Montserrat (www.fsc.ms). Presently, this website is under construction and only local contact information is provided.

Norway

Capital City: Oslo

Currency: Norwegian Krone (NOK)

Official Language: Norwegian

Time Zone: GMT+1

Calling Code: +47

Norway is a highly developed constitutional monarchy occupying the Western most portion of the Scandinavian Peninsula in Northern Europe. Norway is blessed with natural resources including a long bountiful coastline, large forests, mineral deposits and vast oil reserves. The majority of the nation's GDP is produced by industries associated with these resources. In fact, Norway is one of the leading oil producers in the world. Wise investment of oil revenues by the government has given Norway the right to boast that it has the largest capital reserve of any government on earth, adding great financial stability to the country.

It is important and worthwhile to note that Norway is not a member of the European Union. Although Norway is a member of NATO, two referendums on EU membership have both failed in Norway. Norway does not use the Euro either; instead Norway maintains its own currency the Norwegian Krone (plural Kroner, abbreviated NOK). The Krone is allowed to float on world currency exchanges and fluctuates in value over time dependent on a number of factors, not the least of which is the value of a barrel of oil.

Norway, like Finland, is not a traditional offshore banking center, however, like Finland, this country is well developed and does permit its banks to open accounts for non-residents. However, account opening is subject to the policies and approval of the individual banks. Of course, thorough due diligence on the part of the bank will be involved in any account opening.

Banks in Norway are subject to the regulation of the Kredittilsynet, or the Financial Supervisory Authority of Norway (www.kredittilsynet.no). In addition to banks, Kredittilsynet also regulates financial market, investment houses, mortgage firms, insurance companies and other financial businesses in Norway. A complete database of all firms under regulation by the Kredittilsynet is available on their website at http://registry.kredittilsynet.no.

Depositors in Norwegian banks are protected by the Norwegian Guarantee Schemes Act. This act of parliament provides for up to 2,000,000 NOK in deposit coverage per depositor, per institution in Norwegian banks. A complete listing of this law is available on the website of the Financial Supervisory Authority.

Panama

Capital City: Panama City

Currency: Panamanian Balboa & United States Dollar

Official Language: Spanish

Time Zone: GMT-5

Calling Code: +507

Panama is an isthmus nation joining the two continents of North and South America. Panama is most famous for the Panama Canal which, since its completion, has served as major artery of world trade. Originally, part of Colombia, since its independence from Spain, Panama declared its independence from Colombia in 1903. This was done with the assistance of the United States who wished to complete and then control the, failed French Canal project. From its completion until 1999, the United States directly controlled the Panama Canal.

From 1984 until 1989, Manuel Noriega was the dictator of Panama. Amid accusations of corruption and drug smuggling, the United States froze the banking system of Panama. This situation escalated and led to an invasion of Panama by the United States and the toppling of the Noriega government. A liberal government has been in place since.

It is also worth noting that the United States Dollar is the de facto currency of Panama and has been since a mutual agreement was signed between the new government of Panama and the United States in 1904. At that time, the Panamanian Balboa and the United States Dollar were set at par with each other. Since then the two currencies have been circulated alongside interchangeably, although the Balboa is only available in coin form. There are currently no Balboa notes.

The economy of Panama is heavily dependent on a well developed service industry, of which banking makes up a large part. There are currently almost 100 licensed banks and financial companies operating in Panama. Most of these banks and finance companies are of Central or South American origin, however many prominent banks from Europe, Canada and The United States have operations in Panama as well. The banking system is governed by the Superintendencia de Bancos de Panamá (www.superbancos.gob.pa). Most of the information is presented in Spanish, although some English information is offered. On this site you can find information on licensed banks as well as contact information.

There is no depositor compensation plan in place in Panama. However, deposits of less than $10,000 USD are placed in the front of the line for collection in the event of a bank failure.

Panama is also a popular destination for expats from all over the world. This is due largely to the Pensionado Visa Program. This program permits individuals and families that receive qualifying amounts of income from government or private pensions, as well as accrued savings, to immigrate to Panama. For more information, contact your closest Panamanian Consulate.

Saint Kitts & Nevis

Capital City: Basseterre

Currency: East Caribbean Dollar (XCD)

Official Language: English

Time Zone: GMT-4

Calling Code: +869

The two islands of St. Kitts and Nevis lie to the East of Puerto Rico in the Leeward Islands of the Caribbean Sea. These two islands were originally settled by the British and the French in the 17th Century. After a series of wars between the two countries, the islands became a permanent British colony and remained so until the two islands were granted independence in 1983. Today, both islands are members of the British Commonwealth and acknowledge Queen Elizabeth II of Great Britain as the head of state and have a British appointed governor.

Today, St. Kitts and Nevis exist as a federation, with a parliamentary government and stable system of English Common Law. However, over the past 25 years the island of Nevis has brought up the subject of secession on more than one occasion.

Today, tourism is the mainstay of the two islands as is common throughout the Caribbean region. However, shortly after independence the two islands began to develop an international business and finance center with the implementation of encouraging legislation and favorable tax policies (including no personal income tax). Today, international finance, insurance and company registration form the second largest component of the two islands' economies.

The Federation of St. Kitts and Nevis is a member of the Eastern Caribbean Central Bank (the East Caribbean Central Bank is actually located on St. Kitts) and both islands use the East Caribbean Dollar as their official currency. While the island federation is a single member of the East Caribbean Central Bank and has a single seat on both the Monetary Council as well as the Board of Directors, the islands regulate banks on each island separately.

On the island of Nevis, financial institutions are regulated by the Nevis Financial Services Division (www.nevisfinance.com). There is currently only one licensed offshore bank operating on the island of Nevis.

The banks on the island of St. Kitts are regulated by the Financial Services Department of St. Kitts (www.skbfinancialservices.com). A list of licensed bank on the island can be found on the website of the ECCB at http://www.eccb-centralbank.org/Financial/fin_banks.asp. There are currently six licensed institutions listed. Of these, five are either native to the islands or are Canadian banks or are subsidiaries of Canadian banks.

St. Kitts and Nevis were originally listed on the list of Non-Cooperative Countries or Territories by the OECD in 2000. However, the islands quickly responded with legislation and policy implementation and were removed from the list in 2003.

One last interesting fact about St. Kitts is that citizenship can actually be purchased. In an effort to help stimulate investment and development on the island, the government of St. Kitts has created a citizenship through investment program. In this program, individuals who invest as little as $200,000 USD in a qualified government development program are eligible for citizenship and all the accompanying benefits. To find out more about this program visit the St. Kitts Financial Services Department at http://www.skbfinancialservices.com/citizenship.php.

Saint Lucia

Capital City: Castries

Currency: East Caribbean Dollar (XCD)

Official Language: English

Time Zone: GMT-4

Calling Code: +758

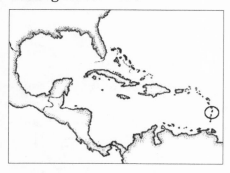

Saint Lucia is another volcanic island in the Lesser Antilles Chain that, like Montserrat, is a member of the Organization of Eastern Caribbean States. Also, like the many of the islands in that group, Saint Lucia is a former British colony. Saint Lucia became independent from the United Kingdom in 1979. Saint Lucia does recognize Queen Elizabeth II as the Head of State and the island is a member of the Commonwealth of Nations. Government and administration in the island is vested in a parliamentary, representative government.

As Saint Lucia is a member of the OECS, financial policy and regulation is carried out through the East Caribbean Central Bank (www.eccb-centralbank.org), in Saint Kitts, in partnership with the Ministry of Finance of Saint Lucia (http://www.stlucia.gov.lc/agencies/ministry_of_finance.htm). There are currently six banks listed as operating within the jurisdiction of Saint Lucia. Most of these banks are Canadian, or are subsidiaries of Canadian banks.

Saint Vincent & The Grenadines

Capital City: Kingstown

Currency: East Caribbean Dollar (XCD)

Official Language: English

Time Zone: GMT-4

Calling Code: +784

Saint Vincent & The Grenadines (Saint Vincent) is an island nation in the Lesser Antilles chain of the Caribbean. The islands lie just north of Venezuela. This island group has been both a French and British colony at times and was recently host to the filming of the popular American movie "Pirates of the Caribbean".

Saint Vincent was granted internal self governance in 1969 and total independence in 1979. Since then, the islands have been struck by hurricanes and volcanic eruptions. This has caused weakness in the economy of Saint Vincent. Saint Vincent also has one of the highest unemployment rates and lowest per capita GDPs in the region. Saint Vincent is also a member of the Organization of Eastern Caribbean States and uses the East Caribbean Dollar as its official currency.

However, in recent years, beginning in the late 1970's, Saint Vincent has made great efforts to develop itself as an international banking center in the Caribbean. Tax incentives were offered to financial institutions that wished to carry out business in St. Vincent. Today St. Vincent has no capital gains tax, inheritance tax or tax on dividends and low corporate taxes by global standards.

Banking laws were overhauled in 1996, with the introduction of the International Banks Act. This Act was revised in 2004 to comply with international banking standards of practice with regard to due diligence and money laundering.

Today the islands are home to six licensed international banks that are required to maintain a physical presence on the islands, as well as submit to inspection annually.

The financial system of St. Vincent and the Grenadines is regulated by the International Financial Services Authority (www.stvincentoffshore.com). Licensed financial institutions, along with their websites can be found at http://www.stvincentoffshore.com/fin_institutions.htm.

Saint Vincent was listed on the original OECD list of Non-Compliant jurisdictions. However, due to new legislations and procedures adopted by the Government of St. Vincent, the islands were removed from all listing and monitoring as of July 2004.

Singapore

Capital City: Singapore

Currency: Singapore Dollar

Official Language: English, Malay, Mandarin, and Tamil

Time Zone: GMT+8

Calling Code: +65

Singapore is a modern city state located on an island at the tip of the Malay Peninsula. This is along the important Malacca Straights. The island's strategic location along this important trade and communication route drew the British to this area in the early part of the 19th Century. The island was officially leased by the British East Indies Company in 1819 and Singapore continued to grow into a thriving community and British military base. The island was conquered and occupied by the Japanese in World War II.

Singapore declared independence from Great Britain in 1963 and became a part of Malaysia. After two years, amid disputes with the Malaysian Government, Singapore again declared independence and set itself up as a sovereign nation. Today Singapore is a thriving cosmopolitan community of more than 4 million people from many different races, religions and national origins all over East Asia. Additionally, Singapore can boast one of the highest GDPs and standards of living in the world. Singapore is also a member state of the Commonwealth of Nations.

Singapore was a large financial center in East Asia before its independence in 1963 and this has only increased since. Today, financial service providers from all over the world carry out operations in Singapore offering services to Asian customers and others from around the globe. All of this is monitored and regulated by the Monetary Authority of Singapore or MAS (www.mas.gov.sg). The

MAS in addition to the regulation of licensed financial institutions serves as the Central Bank of Singapore and regulates monetary policy and issues the nation's currency (the Singapore Dollar abbreviated S$).

As was stated previously, many banks from around the world carry out operations within Singapore, and these banks are permitted to establish depositor relationships with customers outside of Singapore. These banks are divided into two different subsets, local banks and foreign banks. There are currently 6 listed local banks within Singapore, existing mainly to provide services to people residing on the island. There are currently 108 foreign banks of all types licensed in Singapore. Of these, some are industrial banks that are not in the business of dealing directly with consumers, however a total of 40 banks are currently listed as "offshore banks". A complete list of all banks licensed in Singapore is available on the website of the MAS. To discover the specific, current regulations of a particular bank you will need to contact them directly.

Singapore also has in place a depositor compensation scheme which is administered by the Singapore Depositor Insurance Corporation or SDIC (www.sdic.org.sg). This plan provides up to S$20,000 per depositor per participating institution. For a complete list of current participating members, visit the website of the SDIC.

Lastly, in response to the World Banking Crisis of 2008, Singapore has guaranteed all Singapore Dollar and foreign currency deposits in licensed banks on a temporary basis. This guarantee is set to expire at the end of 2010, and is seen merely as a cautionary measure similar to guarantees put in place by Germany, Ireland, The United States and many other countries.

Switzerland

Capital City: Bern

Currency: Swiss Franc (CHF)

Official Language: German & French

Time Zone: GMT+1

Calling Code: +41

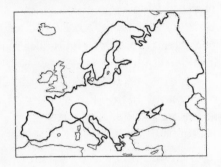

Switzerland is the most famous example of international banking. This landlocked country has a world renowned reputation for both stability and customer privacy. Wealthy individuals, corporations and even governments have often turned to the Swiss banking system for the safeguarding of valuable assets. One of the major reasons for the stability of the Swiss banking system is the Swiss' ability to remain neutral, even through both world wars, while maintaining one of the highest states of defense readiness in the world. The Swiss continue a policy of universal conscription and require members of the armed forces to keep ready in their homes, both a service rifle and a supply of ammunition. Beyond the Swiss reputation for neutrality and defense, the Swiss economy is robust and stable. Switzerland always ranks among the highest in the world for per capita GDP. This too has greatly enhanced the reputation of the Swiss banks.

The Swiss banking system is regulated by the Swiss Financial Market Supervisory Authority (www.finma.ch), or as is it known using its Swiss-German anachronism, FINMA. This organization was created by an act of the Swiss parliament in 2007. FINMA brought under one regulatory body the regulation and supervision of every type of financial services firm in Switzerland. This includes banks, as well as insurance and securities dealers.

The FINMA absorbed the previous regulatory body, the Swiss Federal Banking Commission. All information previously on the website of the Swiss Financial Banking Commission is currently archived on the FINMA website.

The Swiss banking system is host to hundreds upon hundreds of banks from every country in the world. These banks can offer any imaginable financial service from simple deposit account to precious metal storage and fiduciary services. A list of banks licensed to carry on business within the Cantons of Switzerland is available on the FINMA website.

The Swiss banking system is underpinned by strict bank regulation as well as strong deposit guarantees. The Swiss government has mandated that bank deposits be insured up to 100,000 CHF. This was recently increased from 30,000 CHF in 2008, in order to allow Swiss banks to remain competitive amidst the world banking crisis.

Trinidad & Tobago

Capital City: Port of Spain

Currency: Trinidad & Tobago Dollar

Official Language: English

Time Zone: GMT-4

Calling Code: +868

Trinidad & Tobago is an island republic in the Caribbean Sea just north of the continent of South America. The islands were first discovered by Christopher Columbus in 1498. At this time he named the larger of the two islands after the Holy Trinity, calling the island Trinidad. The island became a sleepy Spanish colony after that, with agriculture being the main industry.

During the period of Spanish colonialism, attempts were made to increase the population of the island. Free land was offered to settlers who would swear allegiance to Spain. This led to a large influx of French settlers to the island as well. In 1797, the island was seized by a British naval squadron and the island became a British colony until 1962. In 1976, Trinidad & Tobago severed its connection with the British crown, instead preferring its own elected president as head of state. The republic did elect to remain a part of the British Commonwealth system, however.

Today, Trinidad & Tobago has one of the fastest growing economies in the Caribbean. In 2006, according to the CIA World Factbook, the economy of the islands grew at an astounding 12.6%. This growth is largely attributable to the development of a robust petrochemical industry and the island's large oil and gas reserves.

Along with oil and gas, Trinidad is home to a strong regional banking system. This system is presided over by the Central Bank of Trinidad and Tobago (www.central-bank.org.tt). The Central Bank was established in 1964, shortly after the country's independence and is responsible for ensuring the stability of the island's financial system as well as controlling monetary policy, acting as the bank of last resort, and issuing the country's currency.

The currency of Trinidad is the Trinidad and Tobago Dollar, which is issued by the Central Bank. The dollar is abbreviated with the "$" symbol and is distinguished from other dollar currencies by the addition of the "TT" symbol. The Trinidad Dollar is abbreviated in currency markets with the symbol "TTD". The Central Bank of Trinidad has pegged the Trinidad Dollar with the United States Dollar at an official rate of 1 USD = 6.25 TTD, although on world exchanges the rate tends to fluctuate slightly.

According to the website of the Central Bank of Trinidad and Tobago, there are currently eight commercial banks operating on the island. A list of these banks is available on the website of the Central Bank. Most of these banks are native to Trinidad or are subsidiaries of major North American banks. Foreign citizens can open accounts in Trinidad, at the discretion of the banks. Accounts can be opened for as little as $20 TT.

Trinidad does have a deposit compensation plan, embodied in the Deposit Insurance Corporation of Trinidad and Tobago (www.dictt.org). The board of directors for this organization is composed of members from the Central Bank, the Ministry of Finance and representatives of the banking community. There are currently 24 banks that are members of the plan. Current coverage, for applicable banking products, is set at $TT 75,000.

Turks & Caicos Islands

Capital City: Cockburn Town

Currency: United States Dollar (USD)

Official Language: English

Time Zone: GMT-5

Calling Code: +649

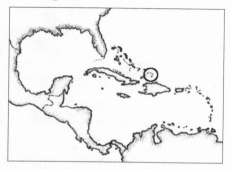

The Turks and Caicos Islands are a chain of islands and cays in the Northern part of the Caribbean Sea, to the East of Cuba and North of the Island of Hispaniola. There are more than forty islands in the group although only a small fraction of these are inhabited. The Turks and Caicos Islands are a popular tourist destination due to their picturesque beaches and excellent opportunities for both snorkeling and scuba diving.

Politically, the Turks and Caicos are considered an Overseas Territory of the British Empire with Queen Elizabeth II of Great Britain being the Head of State. The islands are governed by a British appointed governor and people living in the islands are known as British Overseas Territorial Citizens (BOTC). The capital island of the chain is Grand Turk Island. Due to the island groups close proximity to the United States, the United States Dollar is the official currency of the archipelago.

There have been some overtures from the government of Canada towards a union with the Turks and Caicos Islands. Efforts toward this end began in 1917, with the most recent initiative in 2004. As of this writing, no formal plans exist.

Tourism and financial services make up the majority of the economy of the Turks and Caicos, with financial services accounting for roughly 30%. International bank customers are drawn to the islands due to strict bank secrecy laws (specifically "Confidential Relationships Ordinance 1979") and the fact that there is no direct taxation. Of course, as always, banks will cooperate with criminal investigations including tax evasion.

The banking system in the Turks and Caicos is regulated by the Turks and Caicos Islands Financial Services Commission (www.tcifsc.tc). This regulatory body is responsible for regulation and licensing in the islands. Two types of banking licenses are issued by the Commission. The first of these licenses is issued to local banks for the purposes of offering traditional banking services to people living on the islands. The second type of license is issued to banks intending to conduct international banking services on the island. As of the writing of this, there are seven fully licensed banks that are permitted to carry out international banking from the islands.

Bank accounts may be opened with either domestically licensed banks or their international counterparts. In order to open an account with a locally licensed bank, you will need to visit the branch as well as provide proof of residence on one of the islands in the chain. You will also be expected to submit a minimum of one bank reference letter.

Opening an international account is more complicated because all of the transaction must be carried out via mail. Also, the process is more stringent and selective in order to guarantee that only so called "clean" funds are deposited in the country's banks. This is in place to protect the banking system. Minimum required deposits range from $50,000 to $100,000 USD or equivalent. Deposits can be made in most of the major international currencies.

Vanuatu

Capital City: Port Villa

Currency: Vatu (VUV)

Official Language: French and English

Time Zone: GMT+11

Calling Code: +678

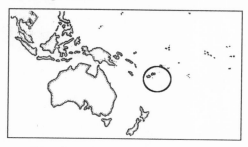

Vanuatu is an island nation in the Pacific Ocean, east of Australia. The nation of Vanuatu is actually made up of 83 small, volcanic islands, encompassing an area of more than 5,000 square miles. Vanuatu has a population of slight more than 200,000 people.

Vanuatu became a joint French and British colony in 1887, known as the "New Hebrides". Vanuatu only received independence only in 1980. At the same time, the islands were granted membership status in the British Commonwealth. Due to the countries colonial heritage, both French and English are official languages. Both of these languages appear on official documents in a manner similar to that of Canada.

Vanuatu is another example of a small country, with limited natural resources, that has constructed a thriving offshore financial center as a means to boost its economy. The closeness of the islands to both Australia and New Zealand has led to a growing expatriate community of people moving to the low tax islands. Vanuatu has no income, withholding, capital gains or inheritance taxes. There are also no exchange controls in place.

The banking system of Vanuatu is supervised by the Reserve Bank of Vanuatu (www.rbv.gov.vu). The Reserve Bank of Vanuatu exercises control over the regulated financial institutions through policies governing capital requirements, exposure, anti-money laundering, relationships between banks and auditors and credit management. The reserve bank also carries out periodic inspections of the licensed banks. There is no depositor compensation pan in place on Vanuatu.

Today there are six domestic banks and eight internationally licensed banks conducting business on the islands. The names of the licensed banks can be found on the website of the Reserve Bank of Vanuatu at www.rbv.gov.vu/VanuatuBanks.htm.

Vanuatu was listed as an uncooperative tax haven by the OECD in 2002 and was the first country on that list to be removed in 2003. Vanuatu achieved this fact through the introduction of information sharing policies in regard to the exchange of tax information. At that same time, Vanuatu revoked or did not renew the licenses of twenty nine internationally licensed banks.

Made in the USA
Lexington, KY
26 September 2013